THE INTENT
Shaping the Future of 'Poverty Economy'

MOHAMED BUHEJI
& DUNYA AHMED

authorHOUSE

AuthorHouse™ UK
1663 Liberty Drive
Bloomington, IN 47403 USA
www.authorhouse.co.uk
Phone: 0800 047 8203 (Domestic TFN)
+44 1908 723714 (International)

© 2019 Mohamed Buheji & Dunya Ahmed. All rights reserved.

No part of this book may be reproduced, stored in a retrieval system, or transmitted by any means without the written permission of the author.

Published by AuthorHouse 10/09/2019

ISBN: 978-1-7283-9245-5 (sc)
ISBN: 978-1-7283-9244-8 (e)

Print information available on the last page.

Any people depicted in stock imagery provided by Getty Images are models, and such images are being used for illustrative purposes only.
Certain stock imagery © Getty Images.

This book is printed on acid-free paper.

Because of the dynamic nature of the Internet, any web addresses or links contained in this book may have changed since publication and may no longer be valid. The views expressed in this work are solely those of the author and do not necessarily reflect the views of the publisher, and the publisher hereby disclaims any responsibility for them.

CONTENTS

Keywords vii
Abbreviations ix
Introduction to 'Shaping the Future of Poverty Economy' xi

Part 1. Redefining the Theory of Poverty Economy 1
Chapter 1   Re-Defining Our Approaches to 'Extreme Poverty'. An Attempt to Disrupting Contemporary Poverty Alleviation Approaches through Inspiration Economy Project-a Case Study 3
Chapter 2   'Re-Designing the Economic Discovery of Wealth' A framework for dealing with the issue of poverty 32

Part 2. Sample of Poverty Economy Projects......................... 51
Chapter 3   Poverty Labs-from 'Alleviation' to 'Elimination and then Prevention' 53
Chapter 4   Eliminating Poverty through Educational Approaches-The Indian Experience 79
Chapter 5   Reviewing-Entrepreneurial Neighbourhoods: Towards an Understanding of the Economies of Neighbourhoods and Communities............... 108

Chapter 6	Discovering Pathways for Eliminating NEET and Youth Future Type of Poverty 113
Chapter 7	Reviewing Implications of "Poverty and Entrepreneurship" in Developed and Developing Economies 146

Part 3. Future Foresight of Poverty Economy 157

Chapter 8	Shaping Future Type of Poverty-The Foresight of Future Socio-economic Problems & Solutions-Taking Poverty as a Context-Beyond 2030 159

Discussion and Conclusion 193

KEYWORDS

1. Behavioural Economy
2. Breakthrough Solutions
3. Educational Approaches to the Poor
4. Entrepreneurial Neighbourhoods
5. Entrepreneurship
6. Extreme-Poverty
7. Future Foresight
8. Humanitarian Assistance
9. Innovative Education Solutions
10. Inspiration Economy
11. Inspiration Labs
12. Low-Income Neighbourhoods
13. Management of Change
14. Models Development
15. Models for Poverty Elimination
16. NEET (Not in employment, education, or training)
17. Poverty
18. Poverty Alleviation
19. Poverty Elimination
20. Poverty Elimination Models
21. Poverty Formulas
22. Poverty Labs
23. Poverty-related Education
24. Poverty Prevention
25. Community Problem Solving

26. Resilience Economy
27. Social Change
28. Social Engineering
29. Socio-Economic Problems
30. Socio-Economy
31. Sustainable Development Goals (SDG's)
32. Types of Poverty
33. Underprivileged Education
34. Wealth and Poverty
35. Youth Economy

ABBREVIATIONS

Consultative Group to Assist the Poor	CGAP
Farmers Income Lab	FIL
Future Poverty labs	FPL
Innovations for Poverty Action	IPA
Inspiration Economy Project Poverty Labs	IEP-PLs
Inspiration Labs	ILs
Multidimensional Poverty Index	MPI
Not in Employment, Education or Training	NEET
Neighbourhood entrepreneurs	NE's
Poverty and Social Exclusion	PSE
Pro-poor growth model	PPGM
Return on Capital Employed	ROCE
Sustainable Development Goal	SDG

INTRODUCTION TO 'SHAPING THE FUTURE OF POVERTY ECONOMY'

Why an Economy for the Future of Poverty?

The economy of poverty is beyond having enough material possessions or income for a person's needs. Poverty is a complex socio-economic, socio-political, legal, technological and environmental issue, to the extent, it still differs from community to community and from one country to another. If we take poverty as a socio-economic issue, it could be seen as an integrated problem that has a negative influence, or negatively influenced from different socio-economic activities such as the lack of: education, cultural synergy, religious harmony and unemployment resolution.

Poverty has been the challenge for many countries, economies and communities. With the rapid developments of 'poverty elimination' efforts, the quest for understanding more about the economy of poverty is increasing from both academics and practitioners of different speciality. Therefore, this edited book comes to give an early attempt about how one international project, called inspiration economy, which focuses on finding opportunities in socio-economic problems as future poverty. This project is trying to the foresight and shapes the future poverty economy, through a selection of eight papers published recently in well-established peer-reviewed journals.

Since poverty has been and would continue to be highly correlated to the issue of human inequalities that limit many people from accessing vital resources and thus participating in the development of their country or community, we need to define such current and future inequality. This is highly essential, if we want future generations to be more resilient and ready for the coming threats of the different forms of poverty.

This book comes in a time where the world is celebrating its massive progress in eliminating extreme poverty and where many people in the world's emerging middle-class yet remain vulnerable to falling back into poverty.

Purpose of this Book

In 'Shaping the Future of Poverty Economy' we try to explore the current and future types of poverty and see in them opportunities now towards major complicated socio-economic solutions. The Inspiration Labs set the framework in how to deal with all the rising situations of poverty, not just to eliminate the current extreme ones. The collection of the published peer-reviewed paper, written and researched by the first editor and experienced by both editors in this handbook is divided into eight chapters. The book tries to cover three main parts that focus first on the poverty economy theory and its influence today and future types of poverty. Then, the reader would be given a sample of field projects that help to eliminate today and future poverty. The third part focus on the future foresighted poverty economy.

Hence, this simple edited book approach poverty elimination from different perspectives with a focus on poverty as an issue that reflects a failure in realising the human wealth and the profound knowledge accumulated in today and future poverty, as illustrated in Figure (0-1). The framework of the book shown in this figure shows that we need to build profound knowledge about the type of human wealth and this need first to be explored and exploited through 'poverty labs'. While if we want to prevent future poverty, we need to foresight the different models of poverty coming for at least 20 years from now.

The editors put forward to the reader a framework of simple approaches, if followed then it would help to shape the future poverty and bring in more beneficial socio-economic solutions for today and tomorrow.

Figure (0-1) Framework for 'Shaping Future Poverty Economy'

Distribution of Book Content

To address the framework and the purpose of this book, it was divided into three parts, as mentioned earlier. Part one sets the basis of redefining the theory of poverty economy to fit the current and foresighted future changes. This part has two chapters. The **first chapter** provides a comparative review and analysis between the approaches of poverty and extreme-poverty solutions, emerging in literature and from the experience of the International Inspiration Economy Project Poverty Labs (IIEP-PLs); carried over three years. The chapter focuses on differentiated solutions of 'extreme-poverty' elimination. Notably, the models evaluated the changes that were carried out from different perspectives which influenced, directly or indirectly, the 'quality of life' of the poor, to keep them away from the poverty line proactively. More diagnosis of the challenges on how to deal with poverty mechanisms and constructs were reflected in different proposed approaches, as part of the chapter discussion.

The **second chapter** talks about the meaning of wealth and how it is related to cases that are leading to poverty. Although the issue of wealth has always been of interest for the economists, the latest developments of the concept of behavioural economy, along with the development of focused socio-economic research in the last few decades, has made wealth more re-visited and explored the subject from poverty economy perspectives. Therefore, this chapter examines the issue of poverty from both behavioural economies driven analysis and inspiration based economy.

The second part focuses on projects done by the inspiration labs to address the future poverty economy. This part is made of three chapters. **Chapter three** about poverty elimination models that are brought along through 'poverty labs'. The chapter shows the current trends of field labs in solving the problems of poverty, today and in the future. The research shows how the focus on the socio-economic perspectives of poverty helps to develop the poverty communities and turns problems into opportunities. The chapter shows how to focus on increasing the production capacity of the targeted poverty community.

Chapter four, comes after exploring all the main types of poverty labs published literature. Thus, this chapter shows the different approaches eradicating poverty through different innovative education services in the poverty areas of India. The research focuses on means for transforming poverty education formula towards 'Capacity vs Demand' rather than 'Supply vs Demand' which would help to improve the quality of the education delivered to the poor with minimal resources. The research involves a thorough descriptive analysis of India's experience in developing a variety of poverty elimination schools, and the alternative educational approaches that could be used today and in the near future.

The third chapter in part two is **Chapter five,** which reviews one of the recent literature written by van Ham et al. (2017) that addresses the importance of 'entrepreneurial neighbourhoods' and its role in eliminating the potential of poverty in different communities. The review shows the importance of multi-disciplinary perspectives when we focus on transforming today and future neighbourhoods, using the spirit of entrepreneurship. This approach is one of the many proactive approaches that could be used for the future poverty economy and which helps in reducing the socio-economic instability, the main cause of poverty.

Another promising future poverty elimination project is presented in **Chapter six.** This chapter shows an alternative solution to future poverty of youth, specifically for those not in employment, not in education or training (called for short NEET). The author presents diagnosis and solutions achieved to this problem by tackling NEET from different perspectives. The research gives a warning signal that this type of problem might unfold to be more complicated in the future.

Chapter Seven blends two important issues: poverty and entrepreneurship. The chapter diagnose again the issue of poverty and its vicious cycles, through understanding the poor environment, status and conditions. Then, the entrepreneurial approaches are evaluated as the alternative solution for coming types of poverty.

The third part which emphasises the need for future foresight of poverty economy to end the vicious cycle that the poor suffer from, regardless if they are categorised in absolute or relative poverty. This part is represented by **the final chapter, Chapter Eight**, which focus on visualising the future coming poverty problems, especially with the fast development of elimination of extreme absolute poverty. The chapter gives a warning about a newly developed type of poverty that is not clearly shaped yet. The book calls for a clear intent to refocus the efforts on the coming relative poverty that is going to be complex, along with more tested mitigation plans.

This confirms the great work of Ravallion's (2016a, 2016b) that emphasised the need of focusing on the social effects of today and in the future, by taking 'relative deprivation' seriously. This means we need to continue to challenge whether the current methods make economically and socio-economically sense for preventing not only eliminating poverty. Lately, poverty economy dedicated researchers, as Ravallion, started to question even whether the current facts about poverty right, or would it fit the future type of poverty elimination. Having the gut to research empirically in the field of how to eliminate the causes of the rising inequality in many growing and emerging developing countries we should ensure that the reality of the quality of life for the majority of mankind, today and in the future. Working on the ground to eliminate the relative deprivation of the poor, or the rising costs of their social inclusion is the main target of this book and its intended coming series.

References

Ravallion, M (2016a). Is the World's Poorest Left Behind? Journal of Economic Growth. 21(2), pp. 139-164.

Ravallion, M (2016b). The Economics of Poverty: History, Measurement and Policy, Oxford University Press.

PART ONE

REDEFINING THE THEORY OF POVERTY ECONOMY

CHAPTER ONE

Re-Defining Our Approaches to 'Extreme Poverty'. An Attempt to Disrupting Contemporary Poverty Alleviation Approaches through Inspiration Economy Project-a Case Study[1]

Introduction

Poverty is a very complicated socio-economic problem that has been existing as long as one can remember, in human history. Poverty complex nature comes partly from the way solutions are proposed to the problem without realising a practical outcome (Buheji, 2018; Newell and Simon, 1972).

More than one-third of the world's population still lives below the poverty level at an average of $ 1 a day. Poverty has

---

[1] Buheji, M (2019), Re-defining Our Approaches to Extreme Poverty: An Attempt to Disrupting Contemporary Poverty Alleviation Approaches through Inspiration Economy Project-A Case Study, International Journal of Economics and Financial Issues, 9 (4), pp. 1-10.

increased with the changes taking place in the world, especially the Arab world (under the slogan of economic globalisation). There is an apparent collapse in the standard of living, especially in developing countries (World Bank, 2019).

World Bank (2018) has set a clear plan to end 'extreme poverty' by 2030 through targeting to reduce those living on less than $1.90 a day. However, to achieve this goal, the world needs at least double its speed in eliminating and alleviating extreme-poverty situations. This requires differentiating and disrupting the current contemporary ones. Boosting the shared prosperity, i.e. by increasing the incomes of the poorest up to 40% does not happen by coincidence, it needs a holistic approach to the 'constructs of quality of life' that engulf the poor.

The literature reviewed in this chapter starts with a definition of poverty and how its theories evolved. The current capital economy approaches with issues of poverty are reviewed along with causes and factors of the phenomenon of poverty. Newly seen factors for the poverty phenomenon were mentioned for reference.

This chapter shed light as part of the constructs of with more in-depth on the mindset of the poor and how it functions are reviewed. Then, capital-based economy approaches to the issues of poverty are compared in relevance to both the latest new socio-economic models that the inspiration/behavioural economies approach brings. The literature shows the influence of the different poverty approaches on the decision-making process. Synthesis of this literature review would be done later to understand what are the gaps in the current approaches and how the lessons learned from the Inspiration Economy Project – Poverty Labs (IEP-PLs).

Literature Review

The literature review target to explore the ways poverty is managed. Therefore, it starts with poverty and extreme poverty as a definition, a phenomenon, a model, and an approach. Studies of the models and the approaches are reviewed in relevance to the principal operations and related interactions.

Reviewing the existing literature helps to segment the different viewpoints of the latest research, in comparison to the IEP-PLs carried out to handle the issues of poverty from different perspectives and to see how they could contribute to speeding up the elimination of extreme poverty.

Definition of Poverty and Extreme-Poverty

The definition of poverty by the United Nations "is a state of deprivation reflected in the low consumption of food and low health conditions and educational level and lack of access to it and low housing conditions." While extreme-poverty or absolute-poverty was originally defined by the (UN, 1995) as "a condition characterised by 'severe deprivation' of basic human needs, including food, safe drinking water, sanitation facilities, health, shelter, education and information'.

What differentiates the poverty vs extreme-poverty conditions is that they depend not only on income but also on access to services. In World Bank (2018) extreme poverty is considered to be those who have income below the international poverty line of $2 per day. About 96% of those in extreme poverty reside in South Asia, Sub-Saharan Africa, the West Indies, East Asia, and the Pacific. However still, nearly half of those in poverty live in India and China. However, as of 2018, it is estimated that the country with the most people living in extreme poverty in Nigeria, at 86 million, then followed by the African Sub-Saharan.

According to the UN until 2015, roughly 734 million people remained under the condition of extreme poverty.

Poverty is seen as a disability of the individual or the family. It is a condition that leads to deprivation of many things and limitations of many necessities of life. This deficiency leads to deprivation due to insufficient income, or lack of income. Extreme-poverty can do even worse.

While poverty is a relative concept that changes from time to place, we might be faced with the perpetuation of poverty over time. Therefore, sometimes, the poor are considered merely as the one who cannot find the strength of his day and night (Schilbach et al., 2016).

World Bank (2019) describe extreme-poverty as something that creeps up, due to wars, conflict, population growth, migration and fragility. Therefore, the world needs many approaches that help to equalise opportunities and improve selective investment in human capital.

Evolution of Poverty Handling

There is a growing interest in understanding the psychology and socio-economic status of the poor and the models that are dealt with them so far. The critical challenge for poverty is that it is rarely been approached from a multi-diversity and multi-disciplinary approach (World Bank, 2015).

Today more focus on the psychological influence and on the way the poor see chances in life and even the way they deal with their available assets. Much focus also on how to increase the incomes of the poor, in relevance to their capacity to develop their resources (Schilbach et al., 2016).

Hence, we need to find more pragmatic business-models that goes beyond pumping resources to the poor and the services of immediate assistance, or direct cash. It is not enough anymore to have pro-poor productive resources. The models also need to go beyond encouraging savings and investments. Part of the new evolution for the models should target to address the needs of discovering opportunities in rural development and in the promotion of poverty elimination clusters that start with the poverty causalities, or in areas where most of the poverty resides.

Types of Poverty and Extreme Poverty

Many types of poverty situations make the mindset gradually adapt to living such a deprived condition. All the types of poverty and extreme poverty, in reality, participate in creating failure in the capacity of the poor to manage their assets or autonomously develop their condition. First, there is the '*financial poverty*', where the poor might have the asset, but not the cash flow. Second to this type of poverty is *physical poverty*, where people would look like poor, or have a health condition that carries the symptoms of poverty as malnutrition.

The worst type of poverty is absolute poverty. It is the same as *the 'extreme poverty'* that the poor reach to be in chronic lack of essential food, clean water, health and housing throughout his life cycle. People in absolute (extreme) poverty tend to struggle to experience lots of child deaths from preventable diseases like malaria, cholera and water-contamination related diseases. Extreme poverty can be found explicitly if generation after generation hand over same poverty status to the next generation. This kind of poverty is usually not common in the developed world.

'Relative poverty' is another type of poverty where the family can be considered poor if it cannot afford vacations, or send its children to higher education. Such people are considered relatively poor since they have no access to government support for food, water, medicine and free housing, they are considered

poor because the rest of the community have access to superior services and amenities.

Then we come to *'situational poverty'* which is about the adverse conditions that occur when natural disasters or human-made wars occur, and people cannot help themselves to be out of the adversity of such situations.

The most complicated type of poverty is 'chronic poverty' which is a situation occurs when there are no seen escape routes out of poverty and people would feel they are trapped with no access tools to get out of such situation.

There is also the *'intangible poverty'* which is opposite of *the 'absolute poverty'*. There are also in certain countries and communities what is called the relative poverty where poor is not really poor as per developing countries standard, but they are poor in relevance to the living standards of the country or the community they are living (World Bank, 2015, 2018a, 2018b).

Today, we can also trace what is called *'temporary poverty'*, which happens due to wars or natural disasters. Then we will have the 'sustainable poverty' where the family members inherit poverty. Finally, there is the human poverty. The 'human poverty' is about the inability of meeting the standard of living in the country or the community of the living. The United Nations (UN) represented by the UNDP, developed to complement the Human Development Index (HDI) since (1997). Recently, the *'human poverty'* started to reflect the extent of deprivation in the developed countries as in relevance to the longevity, the knowledge and the decent standard of living. (UNDP, 2010)

Classical and New Causes and factors of the Phenomenon of Extreme Poverty

Almost half of the world till today live on less than $2.50 a day while 80% of all humans live on less than $10 a day. There are many causes and factors of extreme poverty that have been published in the literature. However, one has to add that these poverty factors are based mainly on the capital-based economy. The repeated factor of poverty that has been with human history is the internal and external human-made conflicts (Newell and Simon, 1972).

Capital-based economy thinkers have always been referring to the family size as a factor of poverty, which not necessarily true. Inflation and economic restructuring programs which led to a different distribution of income or wealth, besides the spread of corruption, crime and bureaucracy are considered other causes. The other type of common poverty factor is illiteracy and low education (Ahmed and Buheji, 2018).

With the development of neuroscience, now researchers are going deeper in understanding the role of cognitive load on the poor judgments and decisions. Studies show now there are many unexploited opportunities to induce the poor cognitive-load by improving their bandwidth of thinking. The good of this approach is that it brings in a unified approach to studying the psychology of poverty (Mani et al., 2013).

Researchers are now focusing on factors in the lives of the poor that are affecting their bandwidth; such as malnutrition, alcohol consumption, or sleep deprivation. Understanding the bandwidth of poor thinking also makes now appreciate and realise why they act or take decisions in specific ways.

The fMRI now helps to capture the brain's bandwidth and thus to perform or under-perform certain essential functions that underlie higher-order behaviour and decision-making. The main constructs of this bandwidth are the cognitive-capacity which controls the poor capacity to solve problems, or retain information, or get engaged in any logical reasoning. The second construct is the self-control, which underlies the poor ability to manage their cognitive activities, Buheji (2017). The availability of this second construct helps the poor to effectively plan, have proper attention to the available resources and thus the maintenance of their capacity to take initiatives or be even alert to external positive, or negative impulses. Mani et al. (2013) and D'Zurilla and Goldfried (1971). Thus, both cognitive-capacity and self-control constructs determine the poor ability to focus, to shift attention, to work with information and memory, and to self-monitor (Marsh and Hicks, 1998).

The imbalance of both cognitive-capacity and self-control in those with extremely poor, influence their capacity to capture opportunities or in creating a change in their poverty situations. For example, one could find that their impaired cognitive function influences their performance in competing in the labour market, especially if the work relies heavily on cognitive capacities such as attention, perseverance, or memory. i.e. this malfunction cognition even influences the performance of a waste picker trying to find valuable items among mountains of garbage (World Bank, 2015).

The influence of self-control also found to affect their nutritional status and thus affect their physical productivity and mental function. Literacy has a great impact on the poor access to the world economy and which helps the poor to deal with loads of information, or instructions more rationally. The absence of self-control leads to many types of addiction, be it alcohol or drugs. These two specifically have long been associated with poverty.

Lack of cognitive-capacity makes the extremely poor spend many efforts on juggling expenses, and compromise in relevance to what they could poorly consume, thus distracting their efforts in making money.

How the Mindset of the 'Extremely Poor' Function?

The brain of the extremely poor is usually constrained. Hence, it cannot establish a causal relationship between poverty and mental function, Mani et al. (2013).

The Intent

The limited functionality of the extremely poor makes him think every day about financial demands. This creates depression such as sleep deprivation and becomes hopeless. World Bank (2015).

The work by Mullainathan and Shafir (2013) about the psychology of scarcity of those being extremely poor showed that feelings of scarcity create more consistent feelings of needs and where the poor would count every small decision as trade-offs. Hence, living this scarcity mindset make the poor focus on relatively simple tasks. In the same time, the poor waste their real scarce resources as their cognitive capacities invested in unnecessary functionality (World Bank, 2015).

Mullainathan and Shafir (2013) emphasised that the scarcity mindset makes life less navigable, as people act in a computationally more complex world. The cognitive-overload imposed by scarcity mindset increases the probability of costly errors. Errors increase the lack of self-control. Thus the poor would fall into repetitive temptations and would enter into 'tunnelling'. This tunnelling causes short-sightedness, making it more difficult for the poor in evaluating the alternatives available to them when dealing with difficulties.

Studies now confirm that the mindset of the poor is not a personal trait, but it is the result of environmental choices produced by scarcity itself. A conservative diagnosis of the mindset of the extremely poor found that it leads them to live with more vulnerable situations. This mindset would make them lack interest in initiatives that could improve their condition.

Thus, as mentioned by Mullainathan and Shafir (2013), the poor would keep delaying paying small utility bills till they need to immediate payment is needed for all the overdue bills, then they would seek help for charity or personal loans, and this feeds the continuity of the scarcity mindset. Another example was given for how the poor would prevent their children from going to school to seek them bringing in some income for the family, instead of trying to compromise between school and work and thus mitigate the risks of negatively influencing the child's life forever (Bull et al., 1988).

The communication in the model needs to be engineered in a way that it would raise the choices of the poor in dealing with social programmes. This means we need to create different criteria's to assist the categories of the potential beneficiaries'. Again the small adjustments in the communication design and implementation of social programmes can lead to very positive changes in their outcomes.

The poor feeding and housing support models should target to give the poor mindset with the minimum of security, so that they would build gradually their temporal horizon, pointing towards possibilities beyond immediate needs. This would improve their decision-making capacity (World Bank, 2015).

'Capital Economy' Approaches to the Issues of Extreme Poverty

The capital economy has brought many solutions to the issues of poverty. Many solutions came with improving the continuous services (depending on the nature of the situation). In the last century, more seasonal services have been developed. However, most of the capitalism efforts gone for emergency services and the enhancement of tools that ensures continuous services for the poor, driven by sympathetic thinking.

The Intent

**Figure (1) Approaches to Poverty Issues
in Capital based Economy**

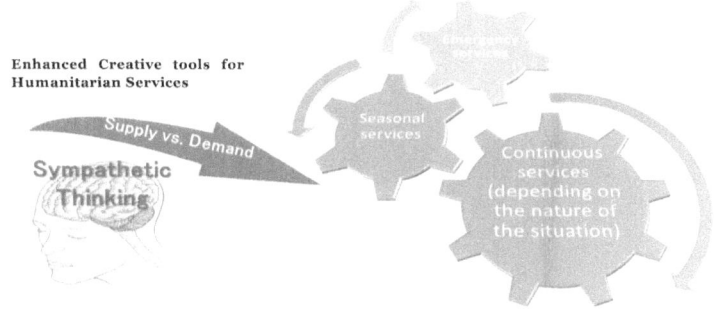

'Socio-Economic' Approaches to the Issues of Extreme Poverty

The total use of production capacities of the poor need to be revived. We need to avoid the causes of migration and ensure effective human development in this class. Currently, the solutions poverty reduction in capital economy focus on developing the labour market for poor employment and then providing them housing services. Other approaches focus on regional development. Also, equality in socio-economic fields is leading to more sustainable development to reduce poverty and improve the standard of living. With the development of endowment projects, more small micro-financing projects started. Figure (2) illustrate approaches to poverty issues from socio-economic perspective.

Figure (2) Approaches to Extreme Poverty Issues from socio-economic perspectives

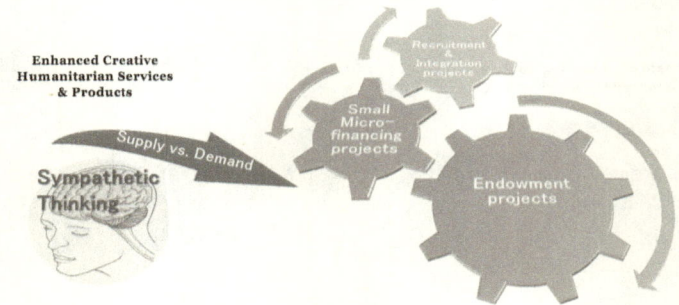

'Inspiration & Behavioural Economies' Approaches to the Issues of Extreme Poverty

Instead of discussing the 'big issues' around 'poverty traps', Banerjee and Duflo (2011) recommended that we should approach the concrete situations faced by the low-income families and communities in poverty, identifying the main obstacles to the improvement of their lives and the alternatives that could be adopted to remove them.

The fight against poverty could be differentiated by the concrete model solutions that change how the poor people, being evaluated, assessed and exploited to great life opportunities. Poor people can be a source for real productive economy, if we change their life focus from focusing on invaluable resources as food for the day, to focusing on assets and wealth of their life (Ahmed and Buheji, 2018).

With the development of behavioural economics and lately, inspiration economy, more projects became focused on creating realised behavioural change in the communities of the poor, D'Zurilla and Goldfried (1971). As illustrated in Figure (3), the poor conditions were more assessed and evaluated towards change. Now the projects are more focused on changing the models that deal with poverty. One of the most experienced radical change was carried to the humanitarian NGOs, where their role is changed from capturing opportunities of poverty and driven by empathetic thinking (Banerjee and Duflo, 2011).

Figure (3) Approaches to Extreme Poverty Issues in Behavioural & Inspiration based Economy

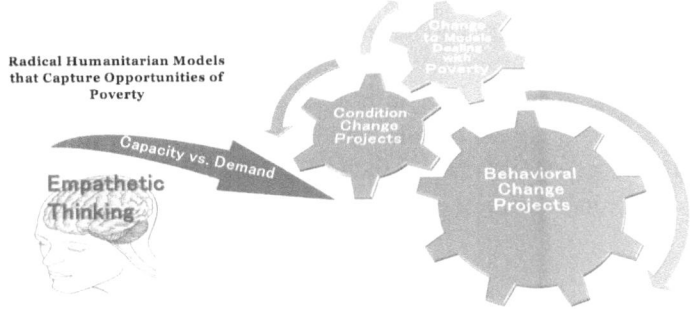

Understanding how the different Approaches of Extreme Poverty influence the related Decision-Making Process?

Understanding the decision making processes that create poverty is very important for empowering people living in poverty. For example, understanding how governments help productive family programs or the effectiveness of micro-start for small family businesses are essential of the value of these social programs in creating a change to people below the middle class. Understanding also how these social programs play a role in creating excessive cognitive, and emotional overload helps us to see how such decision making influence the community.

Such understanding of poverty approaches helps the country to manage the weaknesses of the exposed poor, especially those who are under great pressure and with many uncertainties. Thus, the more decision making process deal with these uncertainties, the more we can help the poor to reach alternatives that can raise their capacity to deal with challenges (Datta and Mullainathan, 2012).

Sometimes just realising small modifications in communication and design in the social programs would create positive changes in outcomes and would help to see successful models that lead to significant transformations. Hence, in order to manage to bring people today to come out of poverty, they need services that are more than reducing the cost of basic needs in all possible ways. i.e. they need inflation more than lowering the level of prices, or providing services in health and housing policies, or reducing the cost of education on their children.

Methodology

The research methodology employed in this chapter is a qualitative case study. The case study was chosen as a method because it is suitable for situations that include complex and multiple variables and processes (Yin, 2003). The case study is longitudinal as most of the examples in dealing with poverty communities, directly or indirectly, were carried for more than six months and operated in different business areas and different countries. The case study is meant to show the differentiated approaches of non-resource based empowerment for the poor and how it can be handled effectively.

The cases were divided into three types of approaches: **'Capital Economy' Approaches, 'Socio-Economic' Approaches, 'Inspiration & Behavioural Economies' Approaches**

The Intent

The different poverty communities' approaches help to visualise differentiated perspectives in dealing with poverty and extreme-poverty. All the data in the table were collected based on the field visits and observations and according to the type of the poverty communities' issues (Buheji, 2019).

The Case Study

The inspiration economy project target is a problem solving focused socio-economic methodology that targets tackle complex world and communities and solves it through using mostly the intrinsic powers of the community of focus. Amongst the most focused upon issues for Inspiration Labs, the field experiments of the Inspiration Economy Project are the issues of poverty and extreme-poverty. The four tables (1), (2) and (3) listed in this chapter show the types of poverty, or extreme-poverty alleviation and elimination projects that targeted to re-define a new way of tackling poverty from a different angle or different perspective. The result of these projects is called models which try to show the re-defined approaches collectively, from the 29 sectors or perspectives. These cases were carried in three years starting from September 2019.

The poverty elimination projects the Inspiration Economy Labs (IELs) focused on sources of poverty and not only resources for supporting poverty. This mindset, which discussed in the literature review ensured that the poverty issue was tackled as one complex socio-economic problem that needed different approaches, Qin et al. (1995). These approaches, in this longitudinal study, are what differentiates the model of poverty issue diagnosis and way of handling challenges in different situations. All these projects were carried out in the following countries: Bahrain, Bosnia & Herzegovina, Slovenia, Morocco, Mauritania and recently in India; where extreme poverty is found mainly in the African countries (Buheji, 2018).

The projects of this case study were divided into four types, which reflect the transformation and integration efforts carried out towards poverty and extreme-poverty elimination. The primary type of projects starts with the efforts of transformation from 'capital economy' approaches to inspiration/behavioural economies' approaches (CA & IBA). The second type of project work on integrating 'capital economy' approaches and 'socio-economic' approaches (CA & SA). While the third type of project work on the integration of 'socio-economic' approach along with inspiration/behavioural economies' approaches (SA & IBA). The fourth type of projects works on the holistic integration of 'capital economy' approaches, 'socio-economic' approaches and inspiration/behavioural economies' approaches Tables (1), (2) and (3) represent each of these types consequently.

Table (1) List of Poverty Elimination Models Projects that integrate 'Capital Economy' Approaches (CA) and Inspiration / Behavioural Economies' Approaches (IBA)

Type of Sector Targeted	Summary of Poverty Communities Related Inspiring Projects/Models
1. Education (CA & IBA)	1-Discovering Inspiring Students at the right time during their 12 years in education. (Early inspiration discovery program). 2-Establishing track of the inspired students after graduation (Inspiration Pathways). 3-Establishing early inspiration discovery program. 4-Establishing Boundary-less Schools that reach the poor to their door-steps
2. High Education (CA & IBA)	1-Improve the academic counselling for the poor 2-Enhance students' fitness or competence to meet labour market demand.
3. Psychiatric Services (CA & IBA)	1-Inspiration of the capacity to manage the anxiety among the poor and avoid reaching the level of chronic anxiety 2-Reduce addiction and suicide ratio due to early treatment of main causalities among youth.

The Intent

Table (2) List of Poverty Elimination Models Projects that integrate 'Capital Economy' Approaches (CA) and 'Socio-Economic' Approaches (SA)

Type of Sector Targeted	Summary of Poverty Communities Related Inspiring Projects/Models
1. Students Socio-psychology Awareness and counselling programs (CA, SA)	1-Sponsoring project on counselling the students' social workers and councillors 2-Simplify tools for measuring poor students' safety or positive psychology, or stress release, or life challenges against continuity in education, even during child labour conditions 3-Awareness campaign for schools and universities, rights for the poor students and reduction school bullying, harassment of the poor. 4-Tackle issues of poor students' depression and see its influence on society.
2. Improve the return of University Courses to the Socio-Economy (CA, SA)	1-Establish a model for Blanket as part of 'Fashion Design Course; in collaboration between the University and the underprivileged women.
3. Anemia Prevention Program (CA, SA)	1-Screening girls in villages for Anemia and link to socio-economic situation and productivity. 2-Set preventive measures for future cases in the community with proper family planning. 3-Reduce the impact of individuals deficiency by addressing the proper diet plans.

Table (3) List of Poverty Elimination Models Projects that integrate 'Socio-Economic' Approaches (SA) and Inspiration/Behavioural Economies' Approaches (IBA)

Type of Sector Targeted	Summary of Poverty Communities Related Inspiring Projects/Models
1. Social Insurance (SA & IBA)	Inspiring the social responsibility plans to ensure that particular type of lower pension jobs is more prepared for entrepreneurship after retirement.
2. Labour Market (SA & IBA)	1-Shifting Unemployment amongst low-income families through building models in specific industries and effective counselling

Type of Sector Targeted	Summary of Poverty Communities Related Inspiring Projects/Models
	2-Raising opportunities for employment through sourcing type for job opportunities, especially in less demanding jobs
3. Humanitarian Services Agency (NGO's) (SA & IBA)	1-Reversing the model of poverty support, by making poverty as a temporary condition that we need to prepare the beneficiaries to beyond this stage. 2-Diverting the type of services to be more for sustained income, instead of non-sustainable support 3-Mapping partnership collaboration services (Academic, youth, NGO's, Government, etc.) 4-Building Cost and Profit centres based on the type of services needed by the beneficiaries, i.e. the low-income families.
4. Woman Village NGO (SA & IBA)	1-Enhance the Return on Capital Employed for the villagers during the chain of making to delivery and distribution 2-Enhance young girls' involvement in Woman village activities to ensure the sustenance of knowledge transfer. 3-Enhancing the corps Return on Investment and profit margin. 4-Setting the type of transformation from distribution to start micro packaging of the high-end product. 5-Improving the quality of life of families in the Amazigh Villages through eco-tourism and small family businesses that support such cluster 6-Build youth independence program that counters poverty through raising the capacity of the farmers for competitive packaging and distribution. 7-Build youth trust in the village system as a source of income
5. Women Entrepreneurship NGO (SA & IBA)	1-Analysing the impact of programs on 'woman development', not only 'women-empower', and the 'living standards' that comes with the 'Quality of Life' in the NGO area and scope of delivery. 2-Optimising the inter-disciplinary learning approach. 3-Enhancing the 'learning by doing' practices 4-Measure the differentiation of women on the economy.

The Intent

Type of Sector Targeted	Summary of Poverty Communities Related Inspiring Projects/Models
1. Poverty Communities Transform-ation Program (SA & IBA)	1-Mitigation of Migration amongst Youth 2-Optimise the Youth Quality Life through Students Pull thinking targeted programs 3-Building a poverty blockage and prevention program 4-Addressing the Gambling (pitting) behaviour amongst youth and building prevention scheme through schools' model 5-Building Youth Entrepreneurship & Innovation programs 6-Enhancing Youth contribution in voluntary work. 7-Bridging the gap between academic Social Work and Social Studies Schools and the realised community problems. (Building Life-Long Learning Programs that shape the Community) 8-Improving disserted women shelters returns. 9-Improving children without known parents' programs 10-Enhancing Red-Cross Programs Impact in the positive psychology of the community 11-Improving Pre-School influence programs on Children of Homeless and Beggars' families.
2. Camel Wool Carpet Factory with a Social Capital & High Community Goodwill-Nouakchott-Mauritania (SA & IBA)	1-Reverse-Design for Wool Factory-Re-designed the model to be from 'Production from the Factory' to 'Production to the Factory' by the productive families and women cells in the villages. 2Re-Distribute Manual Wool Carpet Machines 'from the Factory' focused 'to Villages & Production Families' Focused. 3-Re-establish Organic Handmade Carpet Marketing Program
3. Bringing Low Privileged Community Children to Formal-Education by focusing on Sports (SA& IBA)	1-Integrating youth with both formal sport and traditional games 2-Evaluate possibility for the continuation of formal and informal education. 3-Use peer to peer education.
4. 'Education on Wheels' & 'Education at Door Steps' Projects (SA & IBA)	1-Target to deliver education to rural and isolated communities. 2-Formal and Informal Education for children in slums areas.

Type of Sector Targeted	Summary of Poverty Communities Related Inspiring Projects/Models
5. Improve the Quality of Life of 'Waste Pickers' (SA & IBA)	1-Improve Quality of Life of 'Waste Pickers' Families through differentiating their productivity from Municipalities coming to Waste Management 2-Segregating waste bins implantation in universities, schools & hotels, residential societies 3-Processing of the collected waste into high-end products (i.e. Metals, glass, papers, and organic wastes) processed to high-end products. 4-Improve the Nursery project and ensure the proper distribution channel of Nursery plants

Table (4) List of Poverty Elimination Models Projects that holistically integrate Capital Economy' Approaches (CA), 'Socio-Economic' Approaches (SA) & Inspiration & Behavioural Economies' Approaches (IBA)

Type of Sector Targeted	Summary of Poverty Communities Related Inspiring Projects/Models
1. Social Development (CA, SA & IBA)	1-Inspiring the capacity of the productive family program to be more self-independent and attractive for more family members to join as full-time employees/ owners. 2-Improving Quality of Life of Families in isolated communities and tribes (enhance the productivity factors for women and families working from home), with a target to reduce the impact of poverty through eco-tourism projects. 3-Building stronger family businesses that have higher Return on Capital Employed (ROCE). 4-Enhance the return from Elderly homecare production 5-Enhance the quality of life of the Disabled People and their Production
	6-Easing the process of home care 7-Supporting 'Working from Home' Program 8-Revaluating the Capability of Social Allowance Value and Entitlement – in relevance to Quality of Life with priorities. 9-Enhancing the quality and competitiveness of the product of the Retired & the Disabled

The Intent

Type of Sector Targeted	Summary of Poverty Communities Related Inspiring Projects/Models
	10-Improving the Quality of Micro-Start Families with a focus on Women and People Vulnerability.
2. Labour Fund (CA, SA & IBA)	Divert more mentorship on 'Necessity Entrepreneurship' and improve the solutions they bring to the community.
3. Woman Empowerment Programs (CA, SA & IBA)	1-Closing the gap and accelerating the transformation towards 'Women Development' instead of 'Women Empowerment' especially among poverty and middle-class women. 2-Ensure knowledge sharing between Business Women, Women Entrepreneurs and Women of Productive Families Programs and especially those of the same or relevant business and link it to gamification rating. (i.e. Rating of Entrepreneurs who contribute and share knowledge)
4. Tender Board (CA, SA & IBA)	Diverting more tenders to the benefit of local small SMEs and families' businesses
5. Housing Services (CA, SA & IBA)	1-Reduce the gap between citizens' demands and their quality of life needs 2-Improving the choices and variety of options in non-villa packages (i.e. flats) 3-Reduce the contrary, social inequality and improve social coexistence through post-housing services
6. Police Services (CA, SA & IBA)	1-Reduction of drugs trafficking through refinement and codification of smuggling through reclassification of information in poverty areas. 2-Enhance social harmony between neighbours for small issues among the poor neighbourhood
7. Ministry of Labour (CA, SA & IBA)	1Re-Engineering Counselling Services to start from High School and be Flexible towards Job Creators than just Job Seekers with particular focus on below middle-class families' students. 2-Help start-up companies that collect below middle-class graduate of unique, yet unemployed jobs, that as Nursing, Social Workers, Hospitality Services. 3-Nationalising Jobs that represent the country heritage and support tourism with below middle-class families related to these jobs. 4-Exploring the possibility of creating Human Capital Bank that would transform 30% of the Job

Type of Sector Targeted	Summary of Poverty Communities Related Inspiring Projects/Models
	Seeker towards job creation; over a planned career path. 5-Closing the Gender Gap in Unemployment, by re-inventing new productivity jobs for below middle-class graduating women specifically.
8. Fisheries (CA, SA & IBA)	1-Improve return on Investment (ROI) in fisheries and the resilience in the marines' food industry 2-Bring in the local market of traditional fishers to sustain on the job with their families. 3-Establish National Fishermen Market.
9. Agriculture and Farming (CA, SA & IBA)	1-Redesign Bahraini farmers' production by establishing what is called "National Farmers' Day". 2-Improve the distribution chain of local salad by attracting consumers to purchase local vegetables and fruits, and arranging deals between hospitality suppliers and local farmers. 3-Improve the level of Gardening Competitions.
10. Improve the return of Endowments and trusts (CA, SA & IBA)	1-They are re-evaluating the current assets returns of Endowments and how they are professionally managed to support the people in poverty (directly or indirectly). 2-Establishing 'Sharing Economy' innovative practices and solutions to open more 'Returns on Capital Employed'. 3-Giving an innovative solution for solving problems on disputed family lands 4-Innovating on a type of endowments or trust funds to manage the technical and quality of life developments and diversify the resources in supporting the poverty community.

Findings

In order to understand how the case study projects models Table (1) works and came from, the following Figure (4) framework of diagnosis vs challenges is proposed to tackle any issue in relevance to poverty, or poverty communities. As shown in Figure (1)

The Intent

examples of the early observations from the first field visit shows the assets, or the barriers, or the resources, or the processes that might influence the issue of poverty positively, or negatively, or make it more resource-dependent or independent models. The idea of the framework is to motivate the observations of the 'hidden opportunities' built in the poverty case or issue tackled, and from different perspectives. The proposed framework targets to help us to collect proper information on the problem and thus to generate potential solutions and outcomes.

Re-defining small approaches in dealing with the poor would eliminate the need for concrete solutions faced in their real-life contexts. For example, redefining how we evaluate people income and their functionality can have a drastic effect on the type and level of the poor people empowerment. Also, this framework would help us to effectively evaluate how the poor could target or accept certain jobs opportunities.

Proposed Framework that Guides the Approaches and Re-Define the Models of dealing with Poverty Issues

The framework has been approached the target to re-define any poverty-based model. Part of the goals of re-defining the models of poverty approaches is to enhance the cognitive-capacity. These approaches target to excite the capacity of the poor to solve problems

The different boundaries of the framework in Figure (4) should also address the weak role of the NGOs and the private sectors in dealing with poverty issues. To encourage the new generations of low-income families to become more self-dependent, the framework empowers them to see and exploiting opportunities with minimal resources.

Figure (4) Proposed the way we should Diagnose and deal with the Challenges of the Poverty Models

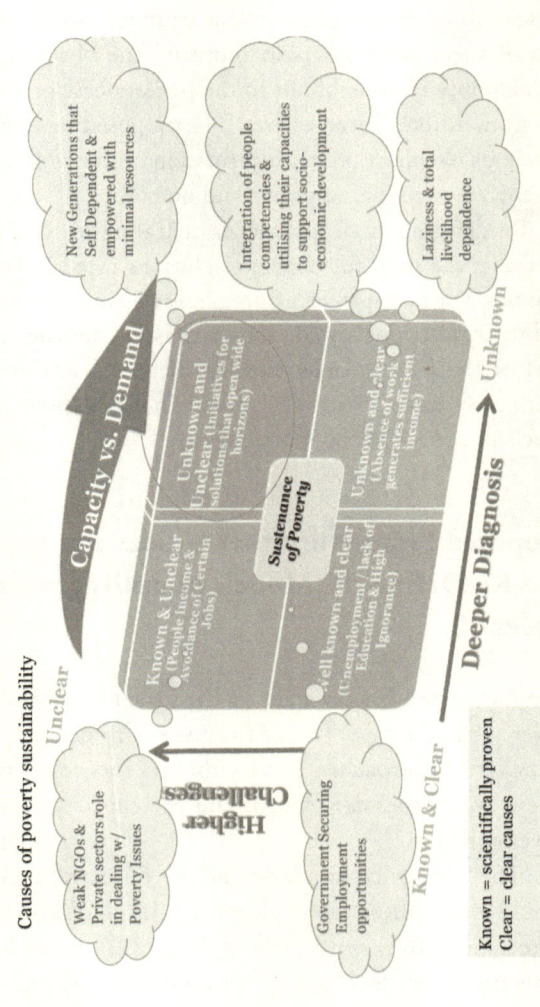

The poverty models are shown in Figure (4) illustrates mostly how the current models focus only the 'well-known' and 'clear' reasons, like unemployment, or lack of education. However, the model needs to address other causalities and in different ways. Indeed, the model should not be dependent on having the government securing employment opportunities for the poor only.

Figure (4) also shows that the model should focus on the unknown and with clear causalities, as the absence of work, which is the source for generating sufficient incomes. Therefore, the models done in the projects address entire livelihood the people in poverty and extreme-poverty usually need to experience or be empowered. This means we need to integrate people competencies and utilise their capacities to support socio-economic development, and this is what Tables (1) to (4) focus on.

Importance of Poverty Model Diagnosis

One of the primary sources of eliminating poverty is the way we diagnose the current poverty model and its causalities. Hence, for example, understanding the decision-making processes in relevance to people living in poverty is only one of the causalities of sustenance of a poverty condition. This diagnosis can lead to the improvement of the poor quality of life outcomes. Some of the main points to be diagnosed in poverty conditions studies are the cognitive and emotional setting, which people in poverty usually subjected to. The analysis of the information should evaluate the accessibility to the limited alternatives that help the poor to deal with their challenges.

Recently, significant multi-disciplined research shown that rational agent models which focus on utility-maximizing behaviour have significant limitations in dealing with a complex problem like poverty.

Type of Approaches to be Re-Defined

Studying the examples of the case study, Tables (1) to (4), shows that small adjustments in the way we communicate with the poor can have a positive effect on how they perceive life. The case also shows that dealing with the poor in the early stages of their life can help mitigate their probability to inherit poverty. In general, Tables (1) to (4) illustrate the importance of designing social programmes with clear outcomes. These small transformations integrate 'socio-economic' approaches and inspiration/behavioural economies' approaches or holistically integrates these two approaches with the capital economy. Based approach illustrates the amount of gap between contemporary approaches and what inspiration labs are suggested to minimise the dependence on waiting for great transformations to happen for the poor from strong external parties like governments, or major fund foundations, or legislative authorities.

In order to re-define the models of dealing with poverty, we need to focus on all the relations and strengths that define the known approaches (i.e. the scientifically proven) and the clear approaches (i.e. the clear causalities) parts, as shown in proposed diagnosis vs challenges, in Figure (4).

Discussion and Conclusion

This chapter aims to extend our understanding of the developments needed in current poverty handling business models and to realise which approaches could help re-define the way we tackle poverty. Taking into account the literature reviewed, the synthesis was done to both the literature and case study represented by Tables (1) till (4) which represent longitudinal work carried over 3.5 years through inspiration and

The Intent

behavioural economy labs that focused on poverty communities needs specifically.

The proposed framework opens up a range of preferences that maximise the probability of behavioural changes amongst the poor community while ensuring the minimum outcome. The case study shows the advantage of the multidisciplinary approaches for a complex issue as extreme poverty. The outcome of the framework proposed to help us to focus on the implications of the models that emphasise the independence of the poor from resource-based empowerment models. The proposed framework helps to develop the socio-economic approaches, programs and public policies set for dealing with issues of poverty, depending on the country's or the community's situation.

The synthesis of both the latest existing models discussed in the literature reviewed and then the models presented as part of the case study realised show that there is a need to re-invent the way we tackle poverty and extreme-poverty. All the current models need to be are re-evaluated on whether they are working to increase the capacity vs demand for the poor and help to develop their self-control. This means we need more projects that would work on the mindset of the poor.

The way poverty models are designed has a significant impact on how the future generations of the poor would be transformed out of their community towards the middle-class. As shown in the case study, this can be done as per the capacity of each community, with small changes, where significant influence would accumulate over time.

The significance of this research is that it would benefit the decision-makers in how to tackle issues of poverty with minimal resources and according to the condition of the country or the community. Besides this chapter is expected to help those engaged with the management of the mindset of the poor and those who need to tackle different poverty problems in preventive rather than reactive way. The chapter is full of examples that open future academic discussions in relevance to the labs, the projects and the policies which trigger the cognitive-capacity of the poor and empower them to solve problems

References

Ahmed, D and Buheji, M (2018) The Distribution of Wealth – Growing Inequality? – A Book Review. Applied Finance and Accounting, Vol. 4, No. 2, August.

Banerjee, A and Duflo, E (2011) Poor economics: a radical rethinking of the way to fight global poverty. New York: PublicAffairs.

Buheji, M (2019) Re-designing the Economic Discovery of Wealth-A Framework for Dealing with the Issue of Poverty. International Journal of Economics, Commerce and Management United Kingdom Vol. VII, Issue 2, February.

Buheji, M (2018) Re-inventing Our Lives-A Handbook for Socio-Economic Problem Solving, AuthorHouse, UK.

Buheji, M and Ahmed, D (2017) Breaking the Shield-Introduction to Inspiration Engineering: Philosophy, Practices and Success Stories, Archway Publishing, Simon & Schuster, USA.

Buheji, M (2017) Understanding Problem Solving in Inspiration Labs, American Journal of Industrial and Business Management, 7, pp. 771-784,

Bull, J., Cromwell, M., Cwikiel, W., Di Chiro, G., Guarina, J., Rathje, R., Stapp, W., Wals, A. and Youngquist, M. (1988) Education in Action: A Community Problem Solving Program for Schools, Thomson-Shore, Dexter, Michigan.

Datta, S., and S. Mullainathan. (2012) Behavioral Design: A New Approach to Development Policy. CGD Policy Paper No. 016. Washington, DC: Center for Global Development.

D'Zurilla, T. and Goldfried, M (1971) Problem-solving and behavior modification. Journal of Abnormal Psychology, Vol 78(1), Aug 1971, 107-126.

Keys, A; Brožek, J; Henschel, A; Mickelsen, O and Taylor, H (1950) The Biology of Human Starvation. Minneapolis: University of Minnesota Press.

Mani, A; Mullainathan, S; Shafir, E and Zhao, J (2013) Poverty Impedes Cognitive Function. Science 341 (6149): 976–80.

Mullainathan, S and Shafir, E (2013) Scarcity: the new science of having less and how it defines our lives. New York: Picador.

Newell and Simon (1972) Human Problem-Solving, Englewood Cliffs, NJ, Prentice-Hall.

Qin, Z; Johnson, D and Johnson, R (1995) Cooperative Versus Competitive Efforts and Problem-solving, Volume: 65 issue: 2, page(s): 129-143.

Schilbach, F; Schofield, H and Mullainathan, S (2016) The Psychological Lives of the Poor American Economic Review: Papers & Proceedings, 106(5): 435–440.

UNDP (2010) Human Development Report 2010. The Real Wealth of Nations: Pathways to Human Development.

World Bank (2018a) Ending Poverty, Investing in Opportunity, Washington, DC: World Bank.

World Bank (2018b) Piecing together the Poverty Puzzle. Poverty and Shared Prosperity. https://openknowledge.worldbank.org/bitstream/handle/10986/30418/9781464813306.pdf

World Bank (2013) Poverty Reduction in Practice: How and Where we work, February 19. http://www.worldbank.org/en/news/feature/2013/02/05/poverty-reduction-in-practice

World Bank (2015) World Development Report 2015 – Mind, Society and Behavior. Washington, DC: World Bank. http://www.worldbank.org/content/dam/Worldbank/Publications/WDR/WDR%202015/WDR-2015-Full-Report.pdf

Yin, R. K. (2003) Case Study Research, Third Edition, Sage Publications.

CHAPTER TWO

'Re-Designing the Economic Discovery of Wealth' A framework for dealing with the issue of poverty[2]

Introduction

Reviewing any socio-economic problem regardless of its nature carries with it default solutions preference that comes from foreseen physical, or materialistic wealth. However, wealth is rarely seen as opportunities and hidden opportunities. With the development of neuroscience and behavioural economics, wealth could be seen, managed and explored from different angles, (Sunstein and Thaler, 2009). Buheji (2017a, b) shown how each socio-economic issue is full of a wealth of opportunities that could be discovered through inspiration economy labs that use socio-economic problem-solving techniques.

---

[2] Buheji, M (2019), 'Re-Designing the Economic Discovery of Wealth' A framework for dealing with the issue of poverty, International Journal of Economics, Commerce and Management United Kingdom, 7 (2), pp. 387-398.

In this chapter, we investigate the 'vectors of wealth' in the issue of poverty, taking it from the perspective of humanitarian assistance and support. In order to come up with an effective socio-economic solution, we need to understand the problem vectors, i.e. its anatomy and the type of opportunities it carries. Problem vectors carry not the only direction for the solution but also quantified construct that carries more than one piece of information. However, studying the best socio-economic solution history shows that the best solution comes from non-financial vectors such as human capital, social and physical assets which help to retain a sustainable wealth of opportunities within each problem. Poverty, even though a complex issue, is no except. It carries inside it many hidden opportunities that need to be explored and exploited.

Therefore, the purpose of this chapter is to explore how we can solve deep, complicated socio-economic problems as poverty through multi-disciplinary perspectives and using the intrinsic powers and hidden assets.

Literature Review

Socio-Economic Problem Vectors

When we investigate the socio-economic problem, we need to explore vectors of growth and development, Nikolaevna and Anatolievich (2015). In order to investigate many complex socio-economic problems, buheji (2018a) stated the importance of using vectors on the wealth of opportunities which each of these types of problems carries within. Resembling problem vectors in physics, as shown in Figure (1) Buheji (2018a) sees that such an approach help to improve the scale of solutions possibility and would make the exploration for problem solution outcome more effective. Realising the problem vector lead to a better understanding of the magnitude and the direction, similar to any other problem in physics or math.

Figure (1) Resemble the Problem Vector Magnitude and Direction

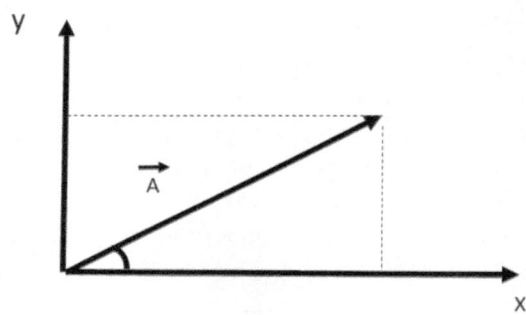

Source: Developed by the Author.

Through the metaphor of the problem vector, accessibility can be observed easily, and integration of the socio-economic issue with different problem opportunities that are considered to be challenging. Buheji (2918a) mentioned examples as to how the integration vectors as the scarcity of space would lead to the redesign of the public buildings, as schools, hospitals and social centres. This created more multi-purpose buildings owned by the community and enhanced the rate of occupancy and utilisation in a small country as the Kingdom of Bahrain.

Selecting the problem vectors of the low utilisation of the public facilities in certain communities while other communities complaining about the non-availability of these facilities, brought the opportunity of integrating of the facilities between different communities and different specialities.

Therefore, problem vector a socio-economic problem vector can be reflected by the following framework where its capacity and efficiency differentiate each problem opportunities to the socio-economic solution expected, supported by the accessibility of the solution and then the other opportunities it brings in, as shown in Figure (2).

Figure (2) Represent the Role of Problem Vector in developing the Scale of Problem Solution

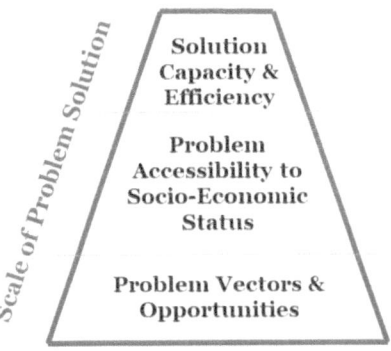

Scope of the Problem

Source: Developed by the Author.

Defining Wealth

There are many definitions of wealth. However, it would take the materialistic one that sees it as the abundance or profusion of anything that has exchange value. Seeing wealth from this perspective, we will see that we have more things in exchange than money or physical assets. We have social assets, natural assets, knowledge assets besides our psychological asset. There are even more assets based on the condition or the environment of the person or the country. For example, we can consider stability is an asset, level of cultural appreciation as an asset, etc.

Ineffective addressing of these assets when we tackle or evaluate the issue of wealth complicates the socio-economic problem further. This has led to many society corruptions that made the target of the decision-makers focused on acquiring the power and capital wealth, at the expense of attempting to develop serious positive outcome-solutions. Obviously, in a sensible world, the government should never undertake to solve community problems, unless it finds that the community cannot solve it themselves, as the more government solve the problems on behalf of the community, the weaker the community capacity would be to solve their own serious problems. This might be especially destructive when governments use resources to solve a problem that they know it would come back again, in the same or different form, after a few years.

The issue of wealth hence, can be visualised through a socio-economic story that develops a solution that manifest 'social functions'. These social functions would establish specific recognized, or intended 'social patterns' which help to re-invent our communities lives and our personal life too. As mentioned in Buheji (2018a), visualising a story of getting out of the poverty for a Barbarian Farmers of al-Amazigh Village in Morocco would lead to capitalising on the village families' intrinsic strengths. This village had unique opportunities of sharing economy practices that manifested and differentiated its social wealth which helped to play a role in attracting its eco-tourism related services.

Wealth in Behavioural Economics

Behavioural economics incorporates wealth from the perspectives of psychology and the analysis of the decision-making, behind an economic outcome; such as the factors leading up to a consumer buying one product instead of another. Thus in behavioural economics, we can specifically propose an architected decision relevant to wealth, taking into account the assets that influence the psychological, social, cognitive, and emotional factors effect on the economic decisions, Sunstein and Thaler (2009) and Cialdini (1998).

Understanding Problem Wealth Vectors

There is scarcity in the body of knowledge about this new subject. However, based on 3.1, we need to always assess the nature and magnitude of the socio-economic problem which entails listing all the "forces", or the "wealth" within the problem that could help us to see, or visualise the desired goals, (Buheji, 2018a; Sunstein and Thaler, 2009). Buheji (2018a) designed a methodology for listing all the intrinsic power resources inside any socio-economic problem. Table (1) is meant to visualise the socio-economic problem outcome through building a story that would link the type of assets inside each problem by describing the Problem wealth, the potential opportunities it carries.

Table (1) Help to Identify the Capacity of Socio-economic Problem Wealth through realizing its assets

Type of Assets inside the Problem	Description of the Problem Wealth	Potential Opportunities	Plan for Outcome Story
Human Asset			
Social Asset			
Physical Asset			
Financial Asset			
Psychological Asset			

Methodology

Based on the above Table (1) type of forces or wealth shall be explored on two selected socio-economic issues relevant to the issue of poverty. Table (2) list the type of forces or wealth within to support the reader to utilise problem vectors effectively.

Table (2) Type of Wealth or Forces Within the Socio-Economic Problem

Socio-Economic Problem	Wealth or Force of Problem
Reduce the gap between citizens' demands and their quality of life needs in Housing services through improving the choices and provision of a variety of options in non-villa packages (i.e. flats).	-Realised Quality of Life Gap for those citizens waiting for Housing Services. -A high percentage of young couples who need special services. -Citizens demands and choices of lifestyle are changing or can be changed to become more resilient and accepting other than villa options.
Enhance young girls' involvement in Woman village activities to ensure their equality in education and sustenance of their knowledge transfer.	-Availability of abundant knowledge from elder village endogenous women that can be disseminated to youth. -Availability of inequality conditions for girls in different countries where they cannot join schools or get enough education.

Application of Wealth Vectors on Humanitarian Poverty Support Services

Brief of Poverty Socio-economic Problem Vectors

The humanitarian services are meant to support people with poverty through different means. However, as one could observe, most of the humanitarian services focus only on one issue, that is the distribution of cooked food along with other materialistic support.

The Intent

Despite many types of sources of poverty, NGOs address people need only through the demand for food and shelter. In the case of the NGO Merhamet, which has semi-independent offices all over Bosnia and Herzegovina (B&H), food and shelter are the focus of the organisation since the Bosnian Civil War in 1992.

There are 300 families with about 600 people who need to be fed every day since they are categorised as families or people 'in need'. Merhamet cooks daily for those dependents a cooked meal, and many families are on the waiting list. Merhamet was targeting to improve its efforts to collect charity or funds to manage or optimise the beneficiaries of these services. Most of those on the list of beneficiaries stay in need of such services until they die. 40% of the NGO beneficiaries are found to be of young age between the age of 16 to 39 years old.

The Classical Solution to such Problem

As many of humanitarian NGO's, Merhamet team would be stretching themselves for finding funds that would address the increasing demands to deliver more meals or service to those families in needs. The team would try to get also sponsorship from the government. Usually, such problem solution increases poverty in the same family as they become more independent on the support of the humanitarian services.

The problem-solvers would start their solution by analysing the ways in which services are provided in relation to the NGO's vision and mission. Then solutions about diversifying the Merhamet services besides the two main meals and financial allowance would be process improved. i.e. Cooked meals for more than 300 people a day and non-cooked food for 80 families a week would be improved, while financial support and clothes (where possible), would be re-evaluated.

Improving the Economic Discovery of Wealth Vectors

In order to come up with an effective socio-economic solution, the wealth problem vectors, i.e. its opportunities of wealth that lead are missed or hidden, need to be analysed as follows:

Understanding the Problem Vectors

The main problem vectors that help to eliminate poverty are identified. The demographics and the role of the humanitarian NGO are also listed as part of the wealth problem vectors, as shown in Figure (3). As per the story, the vectors carry opportunities that can be retrieved from the need to reduce poverty in B&H through effective 'Poverty Elimination Programs' that would block unforeseen poverty enhancement, or poverty fertilization services. This means we need to understand how Merhamet as NGO is reducing poverty.

Figure (3) Problem Vectors for Elimination of Poverty in Merhamet Case

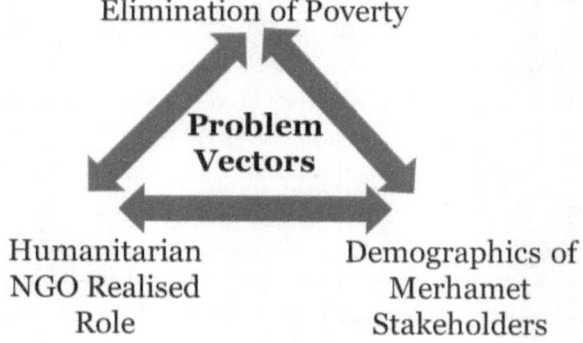

Source: Developed by the Author.

To put the problem in the proper perspective, understanding the current Merhamet beneficiaries and whether they represent the poverty population in the city of Bihac in B&H is a very important problem vector. Besides, it is very important to understand whether the NGO has clear demographics of the beneficiaries and their different assets capacities.

To ensure that the problem is set in the right perspective, we need to understand how Merhamet deals with the assessment of the case and to what socio-economic standards. This means we need to review the families in-need and how poverty or level of wealth is categorised. A thorough review after carrying out a random sampling of the beneficiaries' cases shown that 80% of the families in-need, need to be re-assessed again according to more precise criterions.

A table was established to help detect the priority weight matrix that would measure the special demographics of the poverty cases. Poor families who received two services from the NGO were reviewed again. The reasons for providing cooked food for each family were re-evaluated too. Besides the different updated criteria for eligibility of the services; cases to those families and individuals in-need were categorised as per their age eligibility and functionality. For example, from 60-75 years= green, i.e. most eligible for support. While 59-45 years= yellow, which means have a high probability of being either turned to be out of the waiting list if fit to be trained for self-sufficiency. The rest of ages of 44 – 30 years = red, 29 years and below too, which means these type of individuals should not receive any type of help or support or should receive temporary assistance services.

In order to make each person live with dignity and be fully independent a specific amount was considered as per the following: For a single person = US $35 per week and for a whole family of 4 = US $150, per week.

The Proposed Solution

The problem defined here is about re-considering the best way of dealing with poverty through making the humanitarian Non-Profit or Non-Government Organisations (NPO's or NGO's) work in exploring the condition wealth not weaknesses in the potential beneficiaries and emphasising that poverty food and shelter support realised as a temporary service, not a guaranteed permanent one.

Therefore, the framework of problem vectors discussed and represented in Figure (3) was applied to manage the complexity of the socio-economic issue and accurately use more qualitative and quantitative diagnosis of each vector and what opportunities it carries within.

The first step towards an effective solution was to get youth, from the families 'in need' and cases supported by Merhamet, to get involved in the management of the NGO services. Then a plan was set to building a network that ensures the interaction between those youths and the youths from the donating families. The plan helped to develop a team in Merhamet that helped the efforts in eliminating poverty among the beneficiaries.

The Merhamet team managed to gradually remove the waiting list of those applicants that of 'lower priority' for support while improving the knowledge in those codified as yellow cases, i.e. those 'in needs' but still can be semi-self-sufficient. The observation forms were set for collecting a fresh collection of the socio-economic status data of the families who receive more than one service (i.e. the upper threshold). Criterion such as: gender, marital status, age, ability & functionality, diseases, government support, support from other NGOs, family support, homelessness, financial situation, duration of support from the NGO, number of children/dependents, type of humanitarian services received, transport, were set for defining the weight for each family currently in the support program. The purpose was to

The Intent

define which families are in red and yellow codes that need to be prepared to be out of the list as they are competent enough to be independent and create in fact social and economic contribution.

The problem-solving experts reviewed the codified "green" cases, i.e. those of families proven to be in poverty, in order to reduce their number. The cases on the waiting list were re-examined, and a selection for more families in need as per the weight was admitted to the beneficiaries approved list. Those not in priority for exiting, i.e. those coded as yellow or red cases, were registered for rehabilitation and productive family programs.

The Merhamet humanitarian services were re-engineered towards effectively attempting to minimise the impacts of poverty in the city of Bihac. The extent of the implementation of Bosnia's poverty reduction strategy was analysed to see if poverty really is reducing.

An outline was set for the type of services to be delivered alongside daily meals, depending on the type of functionality of the individual or the family in need. i.e. mentorship programmes for young people, care and cleaning for the elderly and the disabled, etc. A plan was designed so that families would go through a training program that would skill them to cook if they receive dry food, or fresh food. A special scheme program for the homeless led by youth teams was established to be a new scheme of Merhamet.

The response speed for those who apply for help was improved. Different university students and especially those of social studies college were deployed to re-study and frequently assess the NGO's cases every month, as part of an internship program. Plans were set to reduce the number of young people who receive meals from the NGO's service by 20% every year, as they have both the physical assets and functional capacity wealth that make them to contributors not receivers of humanitarian services. The target of Merhamet shifted gradually, over a period of six months, towards reducing the number of those on the waiting list, with higher priority given to those individuals who score less in their functionality. Since the waiting list carried lots of youth, entrepreneurial mentorship support services were enlisted as part of Merhamet new partnership strategy.

Discussion groups at Merhamet started a monthly meeting with youth volunteers. These groups started to implement the different suggestions that help to develop the process of applying, updating and accepting cases. Based on all this progress, the beneficiaries now could be frequently evaluated and assessed for the development and utilisation of their human capital, natural capital (land, property, etc.), physical capital, financial capital and social capital.

A stream mapping to improve "Throughputs and Outcomes" of each family status were started to see the input and the output conditions after training and mentoring services are delivered. The NGO established partnership programs for the development and recruitment of families in need.

The NGO also worked in developing more sustainable funding in terms of finding donors and sponsors, as well as costing the services and then marketing it: i.e. cost to feed a family per day or per year, the cost for bakery, etc. The strategic team started to apply methods that help to consistently move the beneficiaries from being dependent to independent cases, i.e. Cases that do not qualify to Merhamet. This means that Merhamet strategic team would work more on building better 'Capacity vs Demand' based on adjusting the input and output of cases, creating more independence in the Merhamet business model. The project created more pull towards independent beneficiaries: i.e. those who receive their daily meal without support. Yet there is still a need for more checks to be done even for 'green cases', i.e. those families and individuals codified as being 'in need', so that they get qualified towards being more independent.

The Intent

The outcome of Problem Solution

By re-engineering the processes, the list of those 'in needs' in Merhamet has cleared and showed a clear categorisation for those beneficiaries in real need and those that could be moved to the less in need if they were qualified to be more independent. This helped to provide faster services without long waiting lists and made Merhamet ready for any crisis besides raised its capacity for the provision of more relief as a humanitarian agency.

One of the main outcomes of this problem-solving lab is that Merhamet is more confident that it provides services according to real needs. Besides, Merhamet managed to strengthen its presence in the community by building new focused partnerships that helped in accomplishing more effectively focused services. Getting Merhamet beneficiaries gradually coded as (red) and (yellow), which are consistently removed from the waiting list helped to create a model for eliminating the causes of poverty. A development, management and operational teams were established to collaborate together to ensure that these practices are sustained.

A matrix using the weightage table was set to move the conditions and fitness of those in support services from being only 'estimated' to being 'forecasted' in order to measure those really 'in need' and distinguish them from those who should be outside the list. A partnership program based on a win-win scenario was established. The Social Services' College students and the faculty agreed to provide and manage a planned social study for the beneficiaries' cases periodically, as well as providing youth volunteers with the needed evaluation skills.

One of the other main outcomes of the problem-solving lab is that the Merhamet strategic team shifted its focus on improving the livelihoods of its beneficiaries by assessing them in terms of their socio-economic conditions: i.e. through focusing on the different assets and competencies available within each family and thus qualifying most of them to be more productive family. A collaboration plan was set by the Social Development Ministry in the government to improve the situations of those beneficiaries who are unemployed, without household and people who are affected by war.

Discussion

Simplifyi ng the Complexity of Assets of Wealth in Cases of Poverty

Poverty is a complex issue that needs to be tackled from cross-disciplinary approaches so that the sources of poverty are eliminated and the assets of wealth are optimised. For example, if we manage to create more asset of wealth opportunities through exploring, discovering, or restoring or rehabilitating these assets, then we are actually creating more independent individuals or families. Hence, designing the proper channels, within humanitarian NGOs and the beneficiaries in-needs community, would help to ensure the uniqueness of this community and its ability to create a positive breakthrough.

Tackling a socio-economic issue as poverty from a cross-disciplinary perspective helps to bring assets from multiple disciplines to people in-need. Here, the opportunities of the problem solutions, or their outcome, would be reshuffled or re-engineered. For example, observing the way the wealth of the human capital is utilised in the communities or families of in-needs, make us appreciate the lost or the hidden opportunities of wealth in such a category. Hence, governments and decision-makers, including NGOs need to see how they are creating from their services better independent human capital using cross-disciplinary collaborative socio-economy.

Figure (4) Illustration of Cross-Disciplinary Approach for Socio-Economic Problem

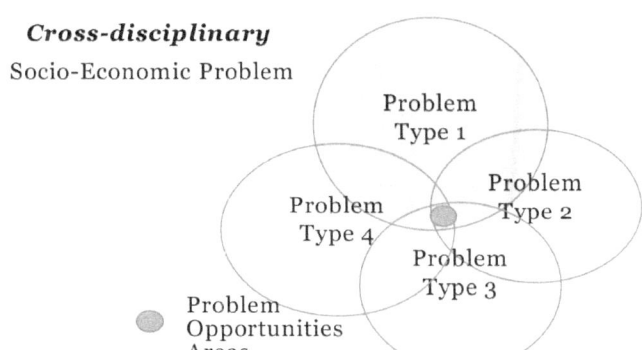

Conclusion

From the case of Merhamet, and what discussed earlier in the tables (1) and (2) including what discussed about the Al-Amazigh village women, one could confirm that the management of the hidden can eliminate poverty or seen wealth of assets and their opportunities through effective counselling of the mindset and self-awareness.

Improving the economic discovery of wealth assets through vectors of wealth problem need to be further studied through the implementation of assessment of further cases of poverty and showing the results of such cross-disciplinary approach on the targeted group of the beneficiaries in-need. More field experiments for such wealth of hidden assets need to be tested in relevance to Levitt and List (2009). The study has one identified one limitation that is carried based on the experience of the researcher and scarcity of literature on the subject. Further studies are highly recommended to develop a knowledge community empirical-based literature that shows problem-solving alternatives for complex socio-economic issues.

References

Buheji, M (2018a) Re-inventing Our Lives-A Handbook for Socio-Economic Problem Solving, AuthorHouse, UK.

Buheji, M. (2018b) The Art of Capturing Opportunities—Screening Arab Social Entrepreneurs. American Journal of Industrial and Business Management, 8, pp. 803-819.

Buheji, M and Ahmed, D (2017a) Breaking the Shield-Introduction to Inspiration Engineering: Philosophy, Practices and Success Stories, Archway Publishing, Simon & Schuster, USA.

Buheji, M (2017) Understanding Problem-Solving in Inspiration Labs, American Journal of Industrial and Business Management, 7, pp. 771-784,

Buheji, M and Ahmed, D (2017b) Understanding the Role of 'Inspiration Productivity, International Journal of Current Advanced Research Volume 6; Issue 3; April 2017; Page No. 2866-2871, http://journalijcar.org/sites/default/files/issue-files/1679-A–2017.pdf

Buheji, M and Ahmed, D (2016) In Search for Inspiration Economy Currency—A Literature Review. American Journal of Industrial and Business Management, 6, 1174-1184.

Cialdini, R (1998) Influence: The Psychology of Persuasion. London: Collins.

Levitt, S. and List., J (2009) Field experiments in economics: the past, the present, and the future. European Economic Review, 53(1): 1–18.

Nikolaevna, L and Anatolievich, S (2015) Economic Research Series, CyberLeninka; Belgorod State National Research University Federal State Autonomous Educational Institution of Higher Education, issue 3, pages 48-55. https://ideas.repec.org/a/scn/032413/16057130.html, accessed: 1/1/2019.

Sunstein, C and Thaler, R (2009) Nudge: Improving Decisions About Health, Wealth and Happiness. 1st ed.

PART TWO

SAMPLE OF POVERTY ECONOMY PROJECTS

CHAPTER THREE

Poverty Labs-from 'Alleviation' to 'Elimination and then Prevention'[3]

Introduction

Poverty needs to be taken beyond economic aspects of the poor people lives, if we are to properly eliminate it or eradicate it from the source. Therefore, in this chapter, we review the definitions of poverty and its main formula's and then shade more understanding of what is meant by extreme poverty. The relation of shared prosperity and poverty alleviation and elimination is also reviewed to set the scene for both the multidimensional poverty measure and poverty cycle. Uriarte (2012).

As the scope of this chapter on economic models of 'poverty elimination' with communities of a limited resource, poverty elimination formulas are illustrated. Types of poverty labs available in the literature and their influence are discussed.

---

[3] Buheji, M (2019), Poverty Labs-From 'Alleviation' to 'Elimination and then Prevention', Journal of Social Science Studies, 6 (2), pp. 108-122.

Example of the 'graduation model', as a sample for the current ways the labs are run, is explored. 'Inspiration economy' poverty-focused labs are presented as an alternative. Poverty as a socio-economic problem is also briefly discussed. Then literature is synthesised and then discussed, before recommendations and conclusion. Buheji and Ahmed (2017).

Literature Review

Definition of Poverty and its Formula's.

There are various definitions of poverty; however, the most widely held definition of poverty measures poverty in economic terms, i.e. the amount of earning in dollars or equivalent. i.e. today we hear the gauge to be less than or above US $2 per day. However, the World Bank (2013) defines poverty as hunger, lack of shelter or access to healthcare, or access to education. Even the World Bank sees that people without a source of income or job, or living one day at a time are considered to have a type of poverty. Thus, poverty encompasses the level of living conditions, or the inability to meet basic needs because food, clean drinking water, proper sanitation, education, health care and other social services are inaccessible.

The World Bank and other poverty-focused organisations defined poverty threshold to be very related to the level of functionality and dependence. Thus, the World Bank developed a measure for the contributors and the causes of poverty through indicators that assess poverty from both income and non-income dimensions. The indicators include education, health, access to social services, vulnerability, social exclusion, and access to social capital.

Understanding Extreme Poverty.

Definition of poverty is shifting as humanity develops, however the basis for poverty stays the same; it is about: security, dignity and safe food and water. When people have very low income and expenditure per capita, deficient consumption of calories of nutrition food, no proper access to food, cloth, shelter, health and education; then they are considered to be extremely poor. Vetterlein (2007).

Extreme poverty is also about not having the ability to come out of poverty cycle such as living in a poor family and being in an environment that makes people highly vulnerable, powerless and afraid, thus feeling that your rights and freedoms are restricted. People in extreme poverty usually live without support, on the sidelines, watching economic growth and prosperity pass by them.

The extreme poverty standard of living can be characterized as the suffering of lack of building relationships, always having to seek out others, or to work for somebody else, unsupported, having nothing to eat, lacking the means to meet clothing and financial needs and having nothing to sell, mostly with restricted rights and freedoms. This would also affect their capacity to make decisions, or to create positive change initiatives.

The World Bank and UN have reported that the world has made tremendous progress in reducing extreme poverty globally to be lower than 10% in 2015. However, there surely today more than 736 million still living on less than $1.90 a day. In a certain region, as the Sub-Saharan in Africa, poverty percentage is increasing, and still, the majority of extremely poor people live, in this region.

Shared Prosperity and Poverty Alleviation.

One of the most developed national models of shared prosperity that helps towards poverty elimination is the Bhutan Government national policy, in relevance to poverty indicators. Bhutan linked its poverty elimination model with what it defined as happiness, in relevance to a sign of shared prosperity, that would come as a result of the integration of the following enhanced per capita income, years of life expectancy, social support, trust on government and freedom to take decisions. National Statistics Bureau of Bhutan (2017).

In another approach, shared prosperity can be defined as the growth in income of the bottom 40% in each country. In 70 of the 91 countries, incomes of the bottom 40% improved between 2010 and 2015. In 54% of those 91 countries, the income grew faster than the average and specifically in East and South Asia. Actually, East and South Asia have managed to bring the bottom 40% to grow annually up to 4.7% since 2010. This progress is followed by both the Baltic countries, Latin America and the Caribbean. However, poorer economies in which extreme poverty rates remain high, particularly in Sub-Saharan Africa, income growth and thus prosperity level remains at the bottom compared to the rest of the world.

As the world grows wealthier and extreme poverty becomes more concentrated; there are legitimate questions over whether $1.90 is too low to define whether someone is poor in all countries of the world. The World Bank now reports on two higher-value poverty lines: $3.20 and $5.50 per day instead of the current $1.90 international poverty line. Data suggest that the rapid gains against extreme poverty have not been matched by reductions in the number of people living below these higher levels of income.

As the world develops, definitions of what constitute basic needs are changing and the same the definition of poverty. If we take, for example, the societal poverty helps to focus the

The Intent

efforts on those considered to be poor, to help them to afford the cost of performing essential society functions. The World Bank has introduced a societal poverty line based on the typical level of consumption, or income in each country. By this yardstick, in 2015, 2.1 billion people were poor relative to their societies, three times the number of people are living in extreme poverty. With over half of the population societally poor, Sub-Saharan Africa has substantially higher rates of societal poverty than other regions. In contrast, East Asia & Pacific has seen its societal poverty rate drop by 38 percentage points.

Multidimensional Poverty Measure.

As we seek to end poverty, we also need to recognise that being poor is not just defined by a lack of consumption or income. Other aspects of life are critical for well-being, including education, access to essential utilities, health care, and security. The multidimensional view reveals a world in which poverty is a much broader, more entrenched problem, underlining the importance of stronger, inclusive growth and of investing more in human capital. At the global level, the share of poor according to a multidimensional definition that includes consumption, education, and access to essential utilities is approximately 50 per cent higher than when relying solely on monetary poverty.

In a sample of 119 countries for the years around 2013, only one in eight are poor in monetary terms, but among them eight out of nine are also deprived in at least one other dimension, lacking education or basic infrastructure services. In the Middle East & North Africa and Latin America & the Caribbean, despite the low prevalence of monetary poverty, almost one in seven people lack adequate sanitation. In Sub-Saharan Africa, more than in any other region, shortfalls in one dimension go hand-in-hand with other deficiencies. Even though South Asia has made progress in poverty reduction, shortfalls in education remain high for both adults and children and are not strongly associated with monetary poverty. Also, the number of people in the region living in households without access to electricity is far greater than those living in monetary poverty.

Poverty Cycle.

Poverty is like a loophole cycle where survival is a daily accomplishment. The cycle size increases when the poor live in communities where those in poverty have no rights. The cycle even deepens when many of those in poverty see education as an 'unaffordable luxury'. This cycle becomes endless since the poor would see only his lack of options, be it for future development, or working with acceptable income (Vetterlein, 2007).

Almost half the world lives with a household income below $2.50 a day. In order to bring people out this cycle, we need to give slight aspiration and inspiration to bring them out their poverty trap. This means we need to equip them to what allows them to discover their opportunities by providing seed capital and encouraging family business and neighbourhood entrepreneurship.

The cycle of poverty expands when we see many people till today, in Africa for example, do not understand the importance of vaccination or making sure of the cleanliness of the water they drink, or at least monitor their health for common diseases and provide hygiene training. The situation of the poor become even worse when living in environmental risk where water supply, housing and land affect their well-being. Vulnerability increases, when people are emotionally and spiritually feel worthless and hopelessness, due to what they experience from poverty.

Poverty Elimination Formulas.

The outcome of any poverty elimination program needs to be gauged by formulas. One of the well-known formulas is 'poverty rate', which is the headcount index, and it is known to be the most important measure in relevance to poverty elimination. It is a formula that measures the proportion of the population that is below the poverty line.

The other formula for gauging poverty elimination is 'poverty gap'. It s an index that measures the extent to which individuals fall below the poverty line, i.e. the poverty gaps as a proportion of the 'poverty line'. The sum of these 'poverty gaps' is index itself that gives those concerned with poverty internationally, or in a specific country, or a community-scale; what is the minimum cost needed to eliminate poverty.

The other formula that is important for those working with poverty elimination models is 'poverty severity'. The poverty severity is an index that combines information on both poverty and inequality. It averages the squares of the poverty gaps relative to the poverty line (Angelsen and Wunder, 2006).

The other formula which is considered very important to the integrity of the poverty gap and poverty average is the 'Growth Bottom 40' indicator. This indicator, which is used to monitor shared prosperity, shows growth in real per capita income, or consumption of the bottom 40% of the income, consumption and distribution in a country. This is very important for developing countries (Aoun, 2004).

Hence, in summary, one could simply understand that in order to count the effectiveness of any 'poverty elimination model', we could measure how much this model can move the poor to the middle class. Currently, the main indicators for this are both 'Shared Prosperity' and the 'Growth Bottom 40'. Thus the growth of in real per capita income, or consumption, of the bottom 40 per cent of the income, or the consumption distribution in a country.

Categorising Types Poverty Labs Available

It is common sense to see types of poverty labs on a scale from correction to preventive. Some labs even might be deepening poverty as they are creating causality for more dependency on external supports, without motivating effective functionality.

Some poverty labs work on the development of poverty cooping services and policies, i.e. developing services that would reach poor from dying, or being sick, or becoming more poor or weaker. i.e. delivering services that do not eradicate poverty from its routes. However, the most popular poverty labs are the 'poverty alleviation labs'. These labs try to treat the disease with a specific mindset, or through a structured approach that has specific measures throughout the world, Uriarte (2012), Japan International Cooperation Agency (2011).

The less known poverty labs are 'poverty elimination' and 'poverty prevention'. Poverty elimination labs mean it would shift many people towards a middle class or at least above the poverty line, while also reducing the 'poverty gap'. 'Poverty prevention' however goes beyond this towards eliminating any causalities that might lead to enhancing the 'poverty gap' or cause any poverty, (Parker, 2010).

Reviewing Poverty Labs Available

Innovations for Poverty Action (IPA)

Even though it does not refer to its work as labs, Innovations for Poverty Action (IPA) work to discover and promotes effective solutions to global poverty problems which are precisely what labs do. IPA designs rigorously evaluate and refine poverty based solutions and their applications together with decision-makers to ensure that the evidence created is used to improve opportunities for the world's poor (IPA, 2019).

IPA works to understand how the proposed solutions work and why it works. This is done by identifying innovative solutions or model designs. IPA labs depend on field replications to evaluate if and how the solution is useful outside of the original context. IPA Labs work to incubate effective solutions. Provide advice and technical assistance to fine-tune the implementation of a solution, ideally integrating it into existing systems.

The Abdul Latif Jameel Poverty Action Lab (J-PAL).

The Abdul Latif Jameel Poverty Action Lab (J-PAL) was established as a research centre at MIT's Department of Economics with a vast global network of 120 affiliated professors and regional offices in Africa, Europe, North America, South Asia, Southeast Asia, and Latin America and the Caribbean. J-PAL's mission is to reduce poverty by ensuring that policy is informed by scientific evidence. It does this by working with governments, non-profits, foundations and other development organisations to conduct rigorous impact evaluations in the field, policy outreach to widely disseminate the lessons from research, and building the capacity of practitioners to generate and use evidence. J-PAL claims that over 202 million people have been reached by the scale-up of programs evaluated by J-PAL and found to be effective. (J-PAL, 2019).

The Consultative Group to Assist the Poor (CGAP).

The Consultative Group to Assist the Poor (CGAP) is a global partnership of 34 leading organisations that seek to advance financial inclusion for the poor. CGAP develops innovative solutions through practical research and active engagement with financial service providers, policy makers and funders to enable approaches at scale. Founded in 1995 and housed at the World Bank, CGAP combines a pragmatic approach to responsible market development with an evidence-based advocacy platform to increase access to the financial services the poor need to improve their lives (CGAP, 2018).

CGAP try to focus on empowering poor people to capture opportunities and be more resilient. Their primary means for empowerment, being the World Bank, is through financial services that collaboration with leading development organisations that work to advance the lives of poor people through financial inclusion. Using action-oriented research, CGAP claim to test, learn and share knowledge intended to help build inclusive and responsible financial systems that move people out of poverty, protect their economic gains and advance broader development goals.

CGAP started recently to use behavioural research that guides policy-makers to predict and take initiatives when they make financial decisions and in the same to make the targeted poor community learn to make better decisions. Even though CGAP (2018) has put a strategic plan for seeing effective solutions through evidence-based programs, they admit that it is not enough for evidence to be used systematically.

Farmers Income Lab (FIL)

Farmers Income Lab (FIL) is another evidence-based approach to overcome collective farmers' challenges, such as enabling small farmers to benefit in global supply chains to meaningfully increase their incomes. FIL work on developing the key levers that most effectively contribute to increasing farmer incomes and models that unlock opportunities for women and lead to increased business value (Farmer Income Lab, 2019).

Influence of Poverty Labs

Abhijit et al. (2015) reported about the influence of Graduation approach that was carried in Ethiopia, Ghana, Honduras, India, Pakistan, and Peru. More than 21,000 people were tracked to test how much their lives and their families' welfare were improved. Abhijit et al. (2015) the project used a comprehensive six components approach over a longitudinal study for over two years. This included the asset to be used for living, such as livestock, or goods to start an informal store, then followed by training on how to manage the asset. The other two constructs focused on: the basic food, or cash support to reduce the need of the poor to sell their new assets in an emergency, with frequent coaching visits to reinforce skills, build confidence, and help participants handle any challenges. Then the last, but not least constructs, were to set to ensure the access to both education and health care institutes that would ensure the functionality and sustained competitive survival of the poor, followed by savings account to help put away money to invest, or use in a future emergency (Markandya, 2001).

The poverty labs research uses even advanced randomised controlled trials, tracking the participants to ensure whether and how living standards are changing during and after the program ends (Parker, 2010).

Graduation Model

'Graduation model' was developed by a consortium of J-PAL, CGAP and IPA that would help to develop more anti-poverty strategies and sustained benefit for the world's ultra-poor.

The effectiveness of the Graduation model approach is that it is a comprehensive approach for those living on less than $1.25 a day. The model evaluates the boosted livelihoods, the income, and the health of this group. The model was tested in six countries, targeting 'poverty alleviation' through a lab that followed 21,000 of the world's poorest people, through a longitudinal study for three years. The data show that this model approach led to substantial and lasting impacts on their standard of living (Abhijit et al., 2015).

Graduation model is in a way like a lab that transforms the focus of just the income of the ultra-poor, to a comprehensive approach that addresses the many challenges of poverty simultaneously, as focus also on having enough food to eat, knowing ways to save, having enough information to survive, besides building positive perception of their opportunities to escape poverty (Abhijit et al., 2015).

'Inspiration Economy' Poverty-Focused Labs (ILs)

Since its inception in 2015, inspiration economy labs (ILs), called for short inspiration labs, focused on solving socio-economic problems in general with more focus on poverty, unemployment, youth, women advancement and migration issues. The uniqueness of these inspiration labs is that they target to find 'opportunities in the problem' and create models that lead 'socio-economic outcome with minimal resources'. i.e. ILs target to create independence and autonomy inside the business model proposed. All this is done through 'unstructured approaches' that uses field data to create radical change (Buheji, 2019 and 2018).

Challenging poverty in inspiration can be seen through more than 30 projects that lead to different models in areas of education, higher education, social development, psychiatric services, labour fund and woman empowerment programs. Also, many works were done in the labour market, social insurance, tender board, housing services and even police services that would support poverty elimination, or create poverty prevention. Greater focus was created towards poverty elimination models through those closest to the poor community, i.e. humanitarian NGO's, woman village NGO's, women entrepreneurship NGO's. Buheji (2019 and 2018).

The influence of the different projects mentioned, lead to the development of different small but essential 'poverty communities change programs', such as the 'camel wool carpets women cells production program' and 'fisheries and agriculture farming profit margin enhancement program'. The effectiveness of the trusts and endowments in changing the situation of poverty were also assessed to bring the purpose of their existence towards the low privileged community. For example, models were developed to bring the poor-families children back to formal-education by focusing on sports and arts. Inspiration labs were also integrated with projects as 'Education on Wheels' & 'Education at Door Steps' and enhanced the counselling of students socio-psychologic capacity.

Recently, inspiration labs are focused on exploring the best models that would improve the quality of life of 'waste pickers', and poor villages societies through productive families' program. Currently, also poverty elimination labs are focused on small selective green-house projects, eco-tourism villages, clean-water management project for villages and anaemia-prevention programs. Also, still, inspiration labs are trying to figure out how to mitigate or eliminate, the migrants and migration risks that would lead to poverty-related symptoms. Buheji (2019 and 2018).

To create all these mentioned model, the inspiration labs practitioners go through a sequence of steps of observing, exploring, learning and reflecting. These steps illustrate the development stages towards an outcome solution for the poverty issue targeted. These development stages are called: codification, classification and stratification, as illustrated in Figure (1).

Figure (1) Model Development Stages during Inspiration Labs

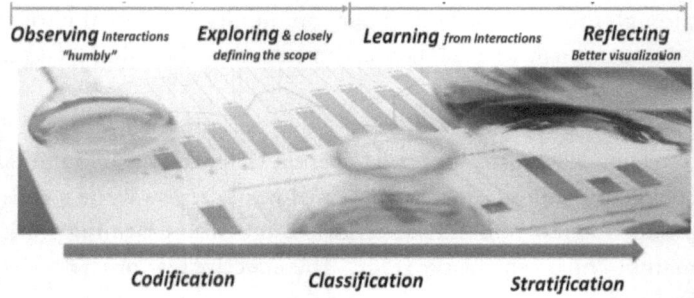

Poverty as a Socio-Economic Problem.

Dealing with poverty as only 'an economic problem' is one of the significant approaches of most of the well-established poverty labs today. Buheji (2019 and 2018) sees poverty as a deep and complex socio-economic problem that needs a scenario for tackling a visualised story, as shown in Figure (2). The clarity of the story would be more once we start a collection for the data and explore more opportunities and ideas.

Then, based on the collection of opportunities exploited, in relevance to the problem, the proposed solutions would be reflected through problem vectors modelling. The refinement of vectors modelling can be developed based on field visits and in-depth observations. Buheji and Ahmed (2017).

The Intent

Figure (2) Exploring opportunities through the development of visualised Story to the Socio-economic Outcome of the Poverty Problem

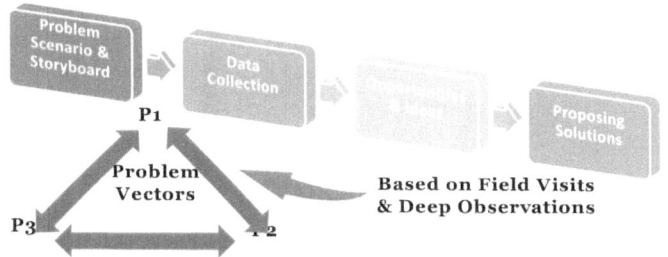

SDG Poverty Clock

United Nations have put poverty eradication as the sustainable development goal (SDG) number one, after failing to achieve the target as a millennium goal (MDG). UN kept this poverty eradication as goal number one. While the current SDG1 target poverty eradication, there is still a gap in the literature that where most of the models target only poverty alleviation. Studies show in specific areas in the world, such African Sahara region, extreme poverty persists. In fact, in order to safeguard people from different poverty throughout their life cycle, we need to develop a variety of unique models in the area of poverty elimination and poverty prevention. As UN published in its official website, to reach SDG1, the world needs even models for that reduce people vulnerability to disasters which we can see even developed rich countries like America, and Japan can suffer from periodically (Markandya, 2001).

The world needs models that focus on those low-income families living on less than US $2 per person a day and ensure that they enter the coverage of the social protection net. The poverty clock shows there is clear evidence for the effectiveness of the UN and massive poverty NGO's methodologies and labs in the reduction of poverty in number. However, compared to the amount of empirical research and funds, there is no clear evidence of how these leaders are working on strengthening the capacity of the weak and less fortunate to enter the middle class. Every year more than 50% of those targeted misses passing the line towards the middle class, due to deliberate actions taken by those in power towards the suggested policies that are tested by the evidence-based labs (Parker, 2010).

Currently, there are still more than 0.6 Billion people labelled to be on 'extreme poverty'. While certain important countries, like India and Indonesia, is on track with poverty with SDGs, many important 'extreme poverty' countries are rising in poverty and specifically in Africa.

Methodology

Based on the literature review a synthesis of the world-leading poverty-focused organisation labs is done to see the direction, the effectiveness and the gaps that need to be addressed compared to the declared intent and the SDG goals.

A comparative study is carried then that differentiate the Inspiration Labs delivery to the issue of poverty in relevance to the great efforts invested by the main labs discussed for IPA, CGAP and J-PAL. The models that came as a result of the inspiration lab unstructured approach are compared to those created models by the poverty alleviation focused organisations (Uriarte, 2012).

Synthesis of Literature

What is meant by Poverty Labs, so far?

Poverty labs hence from the primary IPA, CGAP and J-PAL are representations of research, policy design, education/training and means of financial loans.

The synthesis of the review publications from all the labs show that they all works focused on finding solutions to the world's most significant challenges that lead to poverty; through empirical research and assessment programs. However, the review of the available published literature, including the projects on the websites, shows that none of these labs follows field exploration techniques, in an unstructured way, through piloting and testing of totally different models, in the field, that would move the poor from below poverty line. Even no evidence that these organisations are working with partners or affiliation that conduct attempts towards total new approaches that prevent current models from occurring again and again.

Policy or Models.

No one could debate the importance of evidence-based research for influencing policymakers' decisions. However, one could not see the logic of creating live models that radically moves people in need of financial assistance, or suffering from poverty and its negative effects.

The other issue, despite that all the current organisation labs targets to translates the outcome of their research into action, promoting this among corrupted bureaucratic governments in countries of the south, is another issue. For example, it would be interesting to see how these labs would see the outcome of their work with the government in Africa, or South East Asia, or in

South America; where they sustain reasons for their existence in the weakness of the majority of the society and demolishing of the middle class.

Way of Education and Training in Current Poverty Labs

The focus of almost all the training and education in these labs is to build the capacity of researchers and reports that are evidence-based that might convince the policymakers and the donors to adopt change. Therefore, such training is very far from the poor. One would challenge when such investment in such training and development would reach the poor who might need just small push here and there, or a change of mindset to autonomously correct their life situations. One would argue what the benefit of J-PAL and other labs funds towards open online courses and training programs towards promoting better producers and users of scientific evidence is. How would the poor see this reflected on them? Moreover, when?

Discussion

Avoiding Dependency on the Developing and Under-Developing Governments.

Experience and observation of working as a contracted expert for governments in developing countries and the Middle East specifically governments, follow what could be called 'a show-business strategy' when they are pressured directly and indirectly by international organisations, or advisory firms. Rarely one would experience a developing country government that would take a result of a lab, or recommendation for policy corrections or development and would follow it exactly (Aoun, 2004).

Hence, being dependent on influencing the governments around the world on through policy analysis, or even outreaching them after they ask for help in their social policies us a source of a significant waste for the great efforts and intentions of these labs. It is even unfair for the donors who given a huge donation to benefit the poor in more professional and scientific ways.

Looking for Clear Poor Community Connected Lab.

Most labs work to either empirical study with selected control samples or preparing recommendation based on field experience. What the poverty community needs are more connected labs that show the results on the livelihood of the piloted model and then ensure generalising the model in collaboration with the community itself.

In order to enhance the return of the labs, the community-based model needs to ensure that its influence extends to change the mindset, where the weak assumptions, attitudes, behaviours and reactions would be transformed due to the model implemented or experienced, as shown in Figure (3). This needs, however, the psychology that integrates the soul, the mind and the heart. When both the mindset and the psychology of the poor changes, their thinking would change. Thus their vulnerability to being abused or loss essential opportunities.

Figure (3) Community Connected Model Influence Expected to Change the Poor Capacity

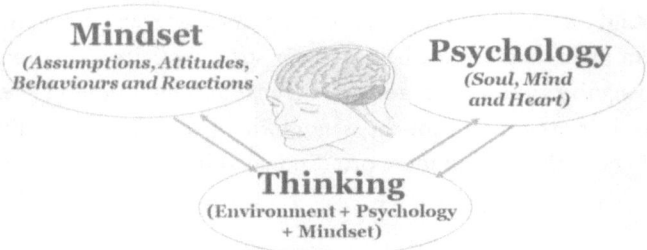

Recommendations and Conclusion

In reviewing the different models of poverty alleviation and the suggested poverty elimination model, the implementation stages towards such models are exploited to the benefit of getting the best practices that would ensure the generalisation of such model creation processes and methodology.

Developing Framework for Unstructured Approach for Poverty Models Development

Based on the analysis of the different labs' work and inspiration economy labs, four stages are recommended towards a useful poverty elimination model that would follow the unstructured approach:

Stage 1-Poverty Elimination Model (Identification Stage)

This stage starts with reflecting on the type of poverty problem and assigning the projects teams. Then, the detailed scope of poverty alleviation project would be more defined through the deep field observations of the type of poverty situation and what type of data needs to be collected.

Stage 2 – Poverty Model Elimination (Implementation Stage)

Once we collect enough field observation, we start discussing these observations and then identify the opportunities inside the specified poverty challenges. Once the different opportunities are linked, a trial and error would be done to ensure that the most suitable poverty elimination model would be produced.

Stages 3 – Poverty Model Elimination (Sustainability Stage)

In order to sustain the influence of the poverty elimination model, the focus on the spirit of the model would keep changing.

These stages need to be flexibly accompanied by the following steps:

1. *Observations are collected during the Site-Visit to Assess the type of 'Poverty Problem' and types of Wealth/Assets Available*
2. *Empathetically Live the Poverty Situation through more in-depth exploration Visit to see how to create influence without or with minimal power and resources.*
3. *Do Brainstorming about the most important Socio-Economic + Then Go to the Field for Data Collection.*
4. *The team discuss how to find opportunities inside the specified 'Poverty Problem.'*
5. *Integration between Opportunities after it is being Identified and Selected to create a Poverty Model Development with minimal resources.*
6. *Implement Experiential Learning (i.e. Trial & Error) until the Poverty Model lead to Moving the targeted Poor towards Middle-Class.*
7. *At this stage, the Poverty Model A formula would be Discovered.*

8. *Defining Type of Differentiation in the Model Developed & Outcome Achieved.*
9. *Building Sustenance & Spirit of Poverty Elimination and Poverty through Pro-activeness related Programs that support the Model.*

Framework for Specifying where the Poverty Elimination Labs Models Should work more.

After diagnosing the type of poverty challenges, we need to see a framework that helps to identify where it fits in the matrix of 'type of problems' and 'type of diagnosis area', as shown in Figure (4). When the poverty problem is 'scientifically known' and have 'clear causality', then our model would be straight forward. The challenge starts when the poverty problem is 'scientifically unknown' and with 'no clear causality', then how the creation of such a poverty elimination model would lead to high economic value. If the model has proven to bring a realised outcome, it could be called a socio-economic discovery.

Figure (4) Framework for Developing Unique Poverty Elimination Models

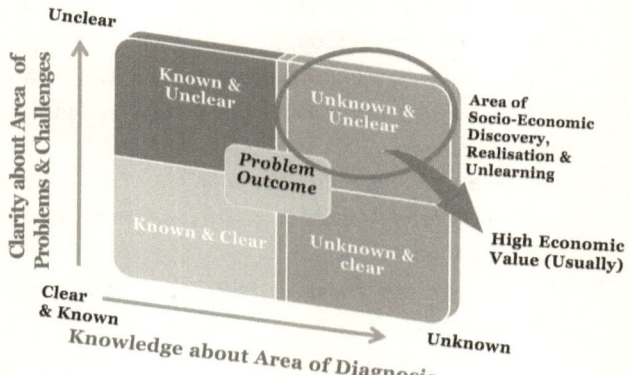

The Intent

Tackling the Mindset of the Poor

It is vital for any poverty elimination model that includes practices and approaches that would tackle the mindset of the poor. The poverty elimination model should ensure that the poor do not surrender to the idea that their poverty is due to their fate and that the causes outside their hands. The model, at the same time, should inspire the poor gradually to see how they can be part of the socio-economic structure. In order to see how they can be part of the socio-economic productivity cycle; the poor people need to be involved, not as recipients of the results of the model, but as stakeholders of the model design. This means that models proposed should bring in more 'learning by doing' facts, such as the various available natural resources in their acquisition that are being disregarded, or under-utilised. Also, the learning by doing would help the poor to discover better productivity tools, or techniques and the opportunity for better learning, rather than just focus on education, for example.

Change of the poor mindset can also come through the actual implementation of what would suggest the benefit for specific and immediate structural changes as re-definition of the poor people right for ownership, be it land, skills or natural capital. Changing also the way the underprivileged can change their rights for social security or loans would also be another expectation from an effective poverty elimination model.

Finally, despite of the limitation of the scarcity of peer-reviewed literature on the development of poverty labs; this chapter set a direction of what should be the aim and focus of 'poverty labs' and what is the alternative to the current models of 'poverty problem solving labs'. The author recommends more in-depth studies in moving labs from 'poverty alleviation' to 'poverty elimination' and then 'poverty prevention'. However, this can't be easily achieved without more field testing approaches as suggested in this chapter.

Reference

Abhijit, B; Duflo, E; Goldberg, N; Karlan, D; Osei, R; Parienté, W; Shapiro, J; Thuysbaert, B and Udry. C (2015) A Multi-Faceted Program Causes Lasting Progress for the Very Poor: Evidence from Six Countries. Science 348 (6236).

Angelsen, A and Wunder, S (2006) Poverty and Inequality: Economic Growth is Better than its Reputation. Chapter in Dan Banik (ed.): Poverty, Politics and Development: Interdisciplinary Perspectives. Fagbokforlaget, Bergen, 2006.

Aoun, A (2004) Poverty Alleviation in the Developing Economies: The Leading Issues. NEW MEDII N. 1. http://www.umb.no/statisk/ior/angelsen_wunder_poverty_inequality_growth.pdf

Buheji, M (2019) 'Re-designing the Economic Discovery of Wealth' a Framework for Dealing with the Issue of Poverty, International Journal of Economics, Commerce and Management United Kingdom Vol. VII, Issue 2, February.

Buheji, M. (2018) Re-Inventing Our Lives, A Handbook for Socio-Economic "Problem-Solving", AuthorHouse, UK. Consultative Group to Assist the Poor (CGAP) (2018) https://www.cgap.org/about

Buheji, M and Ahmed, D (2017) Breaking the Shield- Introduction to Inspiration Engineering: Philosophy, Practices and Success Stories, Archway Publishing, FROM SIMON & SCHUSTER, USA. Farmer Income Lab (2019) https://www.farmerincomelab.com/

Haughton J. and Khandker S (2009) Handbook on Poverty and Inequality. The World Bank.

Ibietan, J; Chidozie, F; Ujara, E (2014) Poverty Alleviation and the Efficacy of Development Assistance Models in Nigeria: An Appraisal. International Journal of Humanities Social Sciences and Education (IJHSSE) Volume 1, Issue 5, May, PP 1-8. https://www.arcjournals.org/pdfs/ijhsse/v1-i5/1.pdf

Japan International Cooperation Agency (2011) Thematic Guidelines on Poverty Reduction. Public Policy Department/Poverty Reduction Task Force http://gwweb.jica.go.jp/km/FSubject1701nsf/3b8a2d403517ae4549256f2d002e1dcc/9418e7cbda6f009a492579d4002a2283/$FILE/JICA_TG_PovertyReduction_2011.pdf

J-PAL (2019) Abdul Latif Jameel Poverty Action Lab https://www.povertyactionlab.org/

Markandya, A (2001) Poverty Alleviation and Sustainable Development Implications for the Management of Natural Capital, University of Bath and The World Bank, Prepared for the Workshop on Poverty and Sustainable Development Ottawa, 23rd January 2001. International Institute for Sustainable Development https://www.iisd.org/pdf/pe_markandya_presentation.pdf

National Statistics Bureau of Bhutan (2017) Bhutan National Poverty Report, World Bank Report. http://www.nsb.gov.bt/publication/files/2017_PAR_Report.pdf

United Nations (2019) Sustainable Development Goals https://sustainabledevelopment.un.org/?menu=1300

Uriarte, F (2012) Poverty Alleviation, Initiatives of the ASEAN Foundation. http://www.aseanfoundation.org/documents/brochure/poverty%2010oct08.pdf

Vetterlein, A (2007) Poverty Alleviation and Human Development in the Twenty-First Century: The Role of the World Bank, Global Governance, Vol. 13, No. 4, (October–December 2007), pp. 513-533.

Parker, I (2010) The Poverty Lab. Transforming development economics, one experiment at a time. https://www.newyorker.com/magazine/2010/05/17/the-poverty-lab.

World Bank (2019) Equity Lab, https://www.worldbank.org/equitylab

World Bank (2019) https://data.worldbank.org/country

World Bank (2019) LAC Equity Lab: A Platform for Poverty and Inequality Analysis http://www.worldbank.org/en/topic/poverty/lac-equity-lab1/overview

World Bank (2019) Global Economic Prospects. Darkening Skies. Report of the Secretary-General, The Sustainable Development Goals Report 2018.

World Bank (2013) Poverty and Labor Brief: Shifting Gears to Accelerate Shared Prosperity in Latin America and the Caribbean.

CHAPTER FOUR

Eliminating Poverty through Educational Approaches- The Indian Experience[4]

Introduction

Nelson Mandela once said, "Education is the most powerful weapon which you can use to change the world". When children in the world and specifically in the mostly populated emerging economy country as India get educated, they can contribute significantly to both the national and international progress. Hence, education is the best answer to poverty and its related issues, like child labour, or early marriage (Suneja, 2015).

Studies show that more than 171 million people could be lifted out of extreme-poverty, if their children get the basic education that would ensure effective communication of reading and writing along with some science and math. This means we would notice an immediate 10-20% drop in the world extremely poor individuals. Absolute poverty could be reduced by 30%

---

[4] Buheji, M (2019), Eliminating Poverty Through Educational Approaches, The Indian Experience Review of European Studies; 11 (3), pp. 32-44.

from learning schemes as per a study outlined by the Education Commission (Kulild, 2014).

A recent Global Partnership for Education (2019) study announced the results of a global survey that show that investing in education increases the earnings of the poor by roughly 10% per each additional year of schooling. For each $1 invested, in an additional year of schooling earnings increase by $5 in low-income countries and $2.5 in lower-middle income countries.

Educational attainment explains the main difference in growth rates between countries as India and the Sub-Saharan African countries, which were continuing to widen from 1965 till 2010. From studying the Indian success story, we could visualise that in 2050, the GDP per capita in low-income countries would be almost 70% lower than today, if we could guarantee that all children would get the basic education and essential lifelong learning skills.

Literature Review

The Challenge of Rural Vs Urban Education in India

Ending poverty requires that the rural and slums areas poverty cycle be controlled and then eliminated. One of the most proven basic controls of poverty is equipping the poor with education. For a country as India, this means more than 800 million who are living in the countryside and in the rural areas of India's out of the total 1.25 billion people need to have appropriate basic education. The rural education services would be more important if we count that at least 216 million Indian are still below the official poverty line with a high increase of migration of such groups to the cities (Suneja, 2015).

With the slowing down of the world economy in general, the urban economy is expected to slow down in India. The rural schools and education system will, therefore, be expected to develop more means to survive and accommodate more coming children; without much dependence on the government programs.

Agriculture is still the largest employer in rural areas. Of the total rural households (90.2 million), over half (57.8%) are involved in farming. Therefore, many educational efforts need to focus on where farmers and their family work and live. The way education delivered to such communities needs to be creative and minimise the cycle of learning that depends on urban-based educational resources. This means we need to go to the grassroots of such farmers' life and exploit the opportunities that would differentiate their learning outcome. This can be done only through civil society non-government agencies (NGOs) which have been and can play a much larger role in this learning cycle.

In order to link education to socio-economic issues of the poor, we need to first look closely into the salient features of their life commitments and lifestyle and what are the actors influencing this situation. Having, for example, an educational program that would transform child-labour to part-time farming would ensure the poor maintain their minimum earnings while they keep their children in education. Knowing that the income of their farmers is less than the US $120 per rural household means we need to enhance the profit margin of the family if we want to keep their children in education programs.

Requirements of Education in Poverty Areas

Achieving realised development and prosperity in India is not just about better farming development, it is about holistic educational packages or programs that would facilitate more entrepreneurship opportunities for the poverty villages, the slums and those even living on the footpaths or in railway stations.

Studies show that the tribal areas in general lag 20 years behind the development of the general population. Still, there are no clear educational packages that would break the poverty of the tribal children, or prevent them from the risk of becoming locked into the poverty cycle.

Having a resilient rural India economy, as Gandhi dreamed of, where people have dignified livelihoods; remains a transformative agenda, that India needs to pick-up on, through innovative solutions. Despite the tremendous success, getting children into school since 2000, almost 60 million children are still out of school, and the decline in out-of-school children has stagnated. The children still not in school are the most marginalised and "suffer" from multiple marginalisation factors and poverty-related issues stagnates in such community. In order to minimise such cases for the next generation, more planned simple educational interventions are expected and are necessary.

Importance of Education to Poverty Elimination

Studies show that any emerging economy country understands the benefit-cost ratios; it would consider education to be the smartest investment. Now we know that for each US $1 invested for schooling in low-and middle-income communities, we would ensure that more student would be on track to gain basic education and would have a higher probability to finish the high school level. Without such investments or specific solutions to replace such influence, the progress toward ending extreme poverty in India would slow down. Suneja (2015), Kulild (2014).

UNESCO policy study paper shows that the global poverty rate could be more than halved if all adults completed secondary school. Yet, new data from the UNESCO Institute for Statistics (UIS) show persistently high out-of-school rates in many countries. Projections suggest that programs that would address

The Intent

adequate quality education suitable for each culture would help to minimise poverty-related diseases, including malaria and AIDs, besides it would improve the family livelihood. Opportunity., E. C. (n.d.).

Education can be the most effective tool to tackle large-scale poverty entrenched in various parts of India. Children who receive holistic quality education are enabled and empowered to grow up into mature, skilled and qualified adults who are eligible for picking up employment or launch their own enterprise.

Recently the newly elected Prime Minister of India Narendra Modi quoted saying "This is an era of knowledge. This is the only potent route to fight poverty. We have to review our commitment to education." SavetheChildren (2017), Suneja (2015), Business Today (2009).

For an emerging and developing country like India, development and upliftment of needy and deprived children can drive the progress of the nation. Education is the key to several issues that magnified due to poverty; such as healthcare, population control, unemployment, besides human rights. Business Today (2009) published that educated individuals are more likely to escape the traps of economic and social despair. On a larger scale, the rewards of individuals getting educated in India found to flow into the entire community, which in turn can have an impact on the entire nation (Suneja, 2015).

Khwaja (n.d.) confirms that an educated community can progress far better as they can achieve better health and robust economic independence. It can see higher levels of homeownership, entrepreneurial activities and improved infrastructure. All this adds up in enabling communities to come out from the quagmire of poverty.

Mohamed Buheji & Dunya Ahmed

Investing in Selective Poverty Elimination Education

Instead of waiting for the Indian government to develop financially supported schemes to covers the extreme poverty areas, this chapter investigates the alternative of selective styles of poverty elimination education, based on tested models. Selective education means we need to develop frameworks and formulas that help to deliver better learning cycles that would reach those children who are disadvantaged due to poverty, instead of waiting for investment from the government to close such gap, which might take a while.

A new research analysis from Nobel laureate economist James J. Heckman finds that early high-quality education has the power to lift multiple generations out of poverty. This new research builds on the evidence showing the importance of a child's earliest years when the brain develops rapidly, laying the foundation for future behaviour, health and learning. Thus investing early in education, as per Heckman, would improve the early childhood experience of the poor students. Education found to reduce the incidence of anti-social behaviour and to break the cycle of poverty.

To help India grow economically, then nothing will work better than helping poor children gain selective quality education suitable for their needed competitiveness. Thus this selective quality education goes beyond just **donating, for example, materials for poor children education** programmes, or paying their tuition from a trusted children's charity. Buheji (2019d) mentioned how selective education provides the best route out of future poverty and inequality. Focusing on the girls' education would help to minimise early child marriage and would improve family planning, besides reducing the maternal deaths.

Selectively empowering the poor by giving them access to information, lifelong learning, coaching and counselling will amplify their possibilities to succeed with differentiation and would prepare them to hold jobs or create jobs or businesses. The targeted selective education should make poor children more confident, give them chances to learn from others and allow them to earn a good living to help their children to live a better life. Such education would be an empowering tool to equip the child or the youth to change the conditions they live in, by taking early actions towards using opportunities around them (Buheji, 2019d).

Since the international community has set 2030 as the date for attaining quality secondary education for all, the gap between what young people want, demand, and believe they have and what they can access will grow even wider. The costs of this learning crisis – unemployment, poverty, inequality, and instability – could undermine the very fabric the socio-economic status of any community. Opportunity., E. C. (n.d.).

SDG of Poverty-Related Education and Wealth Creation

The Sustainable Development Goals (SDGs) encourage the integration of education services that give children the skills of current and future life. Education in poverty areas also plays as a catalyst for different SDGs, since through education we would ensure cross-generational connectedness while resolving household-related issues of primary needs as the availability of: water, food, house, communications, energy, jobs and health.

UNESCO has prepared various papers on poverty eradication within its fields of competence and decided to approach such an issue through a series of projects. During the World Education Forum held in Dakar in April 2000, the international community underscored the need to eradicate extreme poverty and gave its collective commitment to work towards this aim through education, Kulild (2014). Not only is education important in reducing poverty, but it is also a key to wealth creation. Within this context, one of the pledges of the Dakar Framework for Action: "to promote-Education for All (EFA) policies within a sustainable and well-integrated sector framework linked to poverty elimination and development strategies". Buheji (2019a, 2019b).

The role of education is found to be the process which non-financial wealth can be discovered or exploited. This requires a type of education through which even the most impoverished children could create achievements based on their efforts to do projects with learning theoretical to break the cycle of poverty — Khwaja (n.d.).

Hence, by ending the cycle of poverty through education, we could create a mindset for the poor to appreciate his natural, physical, social and knowledge capital wealth. The selective education process would be like an intervention that would help trapped generations in poverty with limited or no resources to see opportunities by different approaches. The outcome of selective education should help to build resources or connections. Payne (2005) mentioned that through education, we would ensure that we would eliminate generation poverty and alleviate situational poverty. Education enhances social mobility where poor students can become more frequently wealthier or achieve higher income than their parents.

Methodology

This chapter follows field observations research which correlates the researcher observation of the ongoing educational approaches and practices in India, followed by the government and many NGOs to eliminate or eradicate poverty through educational services. The research methodology targets to address the purpose of this observational study where the educational means in poverty areas are explored from socio-economic perspectives.

In relevance to the literature review, the process of eradicating poverty in India through education is being explored through field visits and projected on the type of condition of poverty. The direct observations of the way education approaches are delivered in different setting environments and in different India provinces conditions are collected through direct field visits. The cases for the types of observations follow naturalistic, or nonparticipant observations where the researcher has no intervention on the investigated educational environments. Therefore, a procedure of studying the behaviours that are needed for poverty elimination education is followed.

As a naturalistic observation, the researcher did not attempt to manipulate the variables around the poverty elimination education, but focused instead on appreciating what the behaviours needed to eradicate current, and future types of poverty are. The type of poverty area is diagnosed against its type of exploited wealth and opportunities that are supposed to be of focused priority during the learning cycle. Type of programs needed is then specified based on the primary collected data.

The observations are then filtered in the findings stage to exploit what would make the 'poverty and the underprivileged education formula' goes towards selective quality education; i.e. an education that is focused towards 'Capacity vs Demand' rather 'Supply vs Demand'. This means creating a transformation that would help the poverty community children to have 'quality education' with minimal resources and minimal drop-outs.

Data Collection

Type of Data Collected

The field observations collected from the different schools, or various educational means in poverty and the underprivileged areas were possible by the collaboration of with different Indian dedicated NGOs; in Mumbai, Nashik, Goa and Assam, during November 2018 till June 2019. The observations focused on the Indian approaches targeting to speeding-up of the efforts to eradicate poverty, through selective education alternatives for out-of-school children. The observations points focused on the ease of access to schooling approaches. Despite the learning of each outcome of each approach was observed, the researcher founded that reporting such data is beyond the scope of this chapter.

<u>The approaches were evaluated in relevance to:</u>

a. The capability of breaking barriers of the poor reaching the education program.
b. The ability of the approach of building lifelong learning skills that would ensure both poverty elimination and poverty prevention.
c. The suitability of the approach to the conditions of the poor.
d. Whether the approach has 'learning by doing' or 'self-sufficiency' education.

The benefits of each school were also collected, but without exploring more the types of schools under each approach. i.e. there are many types of schools and classes delivery in the slums areas, depending on the type of the area and availability of spaces and funding. Also, micro-financed rural areas schools such as

'Grameen Bank' supported schools were ignored, as it is beyond the scope of this chapter.

The main general note of observation is that not all the approaches have the same focus. i.e. Some approaches as the government and semi-government schools in the rural areas, focus on improving literacy rates among the underprivileged. Other approaches target mainly to equip the children with basic reading and writing capability with some basic math to manage life essentials. We can see clearly this in approaches in the 'School on the Wheel' and some slums 'Door Step Schools'. And there are other types of approaches which are brought by the innovative social entrepreneurs that give the underprivileged child the advantage of disruptive education that would compensate to the limitations of resources that influence or delayed their overall development.

Approaches of Indian Way in Speeding Education to Eradicate Poverty

The following approaches do not cover all the type of approaches playing a role today in India's efforts to eradicate poverty. Approaches as home teaching, education through micro-credits, education focused on the poor access to ICT networks could not be verified, or field visited, however, they exist to a limited scale, despite not being reported as part of the data collection.

'School on the Wheel' Approach

Schools on the wheel is an approach now spreading in many places in India and through a variety of NGOs. The approach addresses the gap in the large population of illiterate children number of India's urban areas. The researchers experienced first the school in the wheel in Nashik, where the NGO is delivering the project target to address a specific tribal community, called 'Sayed community' which more than six generations did not attend any school and mostly been working as stunts in Bollywood. Later the researchers observed the same approach in different cities in India, specifically in Delhi and Mumbai. This approach address specifically urban areas needs where parents are resisting to send children distances of more than 1 kilometre away from the village, or the children being of mobilising families where parents are moving home based on the type of job, or source of family income; as working as labour in construction sites.

This type of approach addresses the need for an immediate solution, or means of education and learning services that can be delivered on-site, to mitigate the risk of having more marginalised children in India that are receiving little or no education. Alternatively, addressing specific children of community high dropout rates. Figure (1) shows the field visits to school on the wheel approach in Nashik.

Figure (1) Illustrates School on the Wheel parking in a shaded area near the tribal huts of Syed Community

'Door Step Schools' Approach

This approach targets to totally break the barriers for poverty areas children who cannot come to school, to be reached by semi-structured school programs delivered by the NGOs. This 'Door

The Intent

Step School' approach usually starts by going from door to door, offering free education services to the poor and the marginalized, then as the number and the trust of the families grows usually the Door Step School takes a settled building from the municipality or donated by sponsors near the slums.

The first known 'Door Step School' was started in Mumbai in 1988, by Rajani Paranjpe and Bina Lashkari in Mumbai, India. Since then this approach spread all over India, and even copied by many leading international NGOs, in different countries with similar issues of poverty, where educational access to the poor and marginalised is still a challenge. Despite the many efforts undertaken by the government and leading Indian private enterprises and NGOs, there are about 1.7 million children might benefit from such an approach.

The 'Door Step School' approach usually addresses the challenge of the slums where there are many children dropout and with many challenges of completing their education through formal government schools, or deprived of being to coop with education programs that don't realise the needs and the limitations of the families where parents can't coop with daily labour and taking care of younger siblings while at work.

The uniqueness of the 'Door Step School' approach, compared to other observed approaches in this study, is that have more capacity in bridging the gap towards the SDGs and the Indian government educational plans in relevant to the underprivileged and enhancement of sustained schools' enrolment rates. Figure (2) shows visits of the researcher to two different slums 'Door Step School' programs in a Mumbai and Assam slums.

Figure (2) Illustrates 'Door Step School' visits on two different slums areas in Mumbai and Assam

'Government Supported School' Approach

Rural education in India is of importance to the government as the majority of India's children lives in villages. Kaur (2019) report that despite that the number of rural students attending schools is rising, more than half of the students in fifth grade are unable to read a second-grade textbook or are not able to solve simple math problems.

The observation of the visited rural schools is that they are not evenly distributed as per the population and areas. For example, not every village have schools. The quality access to suitable education is creating major concern in rural schools. Such government supported rural schools approach found to have fewer committed teachers and lack of in proper textbooks. Figure (3) show an example of how government-supported rural schools in India are mostly overly packed with students, with high students: teacher ratio.

Figure (3) Illustrates Government Supported Schools in rural areas in Assam, where the poor can afford to bring their children to formal education and the school classes would be overcrowded

'Semi-Government Supported Schools' Approach

Semi-government supported schools found to be physically not as good as fully supported schools. Such schools still suffer from high students drop-out, besides being weak in English teaching. The other observation noted, is that the education curriculum is not related to the rural type of culture, traditions and values. The teaching does not take account of students' inclusion programs, extracurricular classes and the different students 'learning difficulties'.

These are other innovative and successful examples of schools running in rural India. It is the time to replicate such efforts in India, and its rural population is growing very vast and which means more schools are required in these areas. Therefore, the timely assessment of rural schools needs will throw light on present problems and achievements.

Figure (4) Illustrates Government Semi-Supported Schools in rural areas in Assam, where the school would have very limited resources to deliver formal education

NGOs Managed Schools

There are a variety of goals that were observed for the different non-government organisations (NGOs) managed schools in India's poverty community, be it a charity-driven, or a community change-focused organisation. However, one of the main consistent observations was improving students' attendance and continuation of education by focusing on physically get them to the class in the first place. The main differentiation of the NGOs managed approaches, particularly in rural areas and in the slums, is that they have a good high rate of elimination of children drop out, especially those below high school. They are more trusted to convince the families to see alternatives or the positives of keeping the child finish the minimal primary basic education classes.

Many of the NGOs supported educational schemes create services mix to encourage families to make their children attend most days of school as giving financial support, or get food, or receive regular health check-ups. Figure (5) shows the crowdiness of the NGOs fully managed schools, yet with high students' attendance.

The Intent

Figure (5) Illustrates NGO fully managed School in rural areas in Assam, striving to deliver formal education with simple construction and overcrowded students

Innovative Disruptive Education (Structured & Unstructured peer to peer education) Schools Approach (Akshar Model)

Akshar is one of the unique, simple, innovative, disruptive educational approaches that are focused on improving the level of educational outcome delivered to the underprivileged through strong educational initiatives led by the NGOs and social entrepreneurs in India. Akshar target to close the gap of the children from low-income families through building on the unique learning capacities that would help them to coop with life challenges and make a difference. The peer-t0-peer approach and modular learning based on the one to one teaching targets to increase the hit rate of the Akshar students to be unique in both theory and practice. This program is similar to programs experienced by the researcher called 'experiential learning' approach, which was excluded in this study due to its being tested in leading schools and not necessarily address the poor needs.

Figure (6) shows the Akshar model delivered in the suburbs of the Guwahati in Assam.

Figure (6) Illustrates one of the Innovative Disruptive Education Model School approach, usually led by Social Entrepreneurs. This model called Akshar is delivered in the Capital of Assam, Guwahati

Findings

General Findings

The observed data collected on the poverty elimination educational approaches shows that there are no links between these educational approaches and the wealth of assets of the poverty area served. The data shows there could a link between the approaches and the barriers of the poor towards education.

The finding shows that the approaches have a different level of influence on the lifelong learning skills of the students. Some approaches have more learning by doing educational practices than others. Mainly only one approach, called Akshar, encourage self-sufficiency mindset.

The Intent

Poverty Elimination Educational Approaches and Type of Wealth

As mentioned in 6.1, the poverty elimination approaches do not seem to have any linkage currently with both the poverty area where the school or the classes are delivered, and the wealth of possible assets that the poor students could be inspired to use, or to change their current situation. In Table (1) we try to link the three variables, re-organised from the scattered field observations to see how to enhance the capacity of the educational services, delivered to the poor by the six different approaches mentioned in this study, to exploit the poor wealth of asset and hidden opportunities.

Table (1) Possible Missing Relations between the Type of poverty area along with the possible assets and opportunities of wealth with the educational Approaches needed

Type of Poverty Area	Wealth & Focus Priority	Type of Educational Approach Needed
Fisheries Areas	Physical, Natural, Knowledge Assets	-Door Step Schools -Home teaching -Semi-Government Supported Schools
Agriculture Areas	Natural, Physical and Knowledge Assets	-Microcredit Schools -Semi-Government Supported Schools
Remote Areas (areas between main cities)	Physical and Non-Financial Assets, then Natural Assets	-Home Teaching -Microcredit Schools -Disruptive Learning & Peer-to-Peer Schools -Government Supported Schools

Type of Poverty Area	Wealth & Focus Priority	Type of Educational Approach Needed
Mountaineers Areas	Physical, Natural and Knowledge Assets	-Missionary Christian Schools -Door Step Schools -Semi-Government Supported Schools
Slums Areas in Main Cities	Knowledge, then Physical and Non-Financial Assets	-Slums Schools -Door Step Schools -Disruptive Learning & Peer-to-Peer Schools -Teaching on the Wheel Schools -Semi-Government Supported Schools -ICT focused schools

Influence of Current Educational Approaches on the Poor Mindset

Since the scope of this chapter about the educational approaches that are available in India today to eliminate poverty, one could not undermine evaluating the influence of such approaches on the mindset of the poor. Buheji (2019) mentioned that without changing the mindset of the poor children, we could not guarantee that they would escape from the vicious poverty trap. Therefore, we need a type of education that would change the assumptions, the perception, the attitudes, the behaviours and the reactions of these underprivileged children and youth, in relevance to their possible wealth alternatives and opportunities. Going through the six approaches and their way of delivery, none of them could claim they are directly contributing to this level of mindset change.

To be accurate and precise, Akshar may follow a mild multi-disciplined approach to a certain extent. However, again, all the approaches miss clear programs that would lead to a holistic

The Intent

mindset that would start to see and exploit opportunities around the challenges faced in life. The absence of the multi-disciplined innovative teaching approaches that fit the environment and the condition of the poor condition student in the underprivileged community is actually a serious gap that needs to be rectified if India and similar countries want to reach the SDGs with a competent generation that could see the opportunities in the problems. Figure (7) reflects the type of mindset driven education needed by the underprivileged students today, as mentioned in Buheji (2018).

Figure (7) Levels of Mindset Possibilities Needed in the Poverty Elimination Educational Approaches

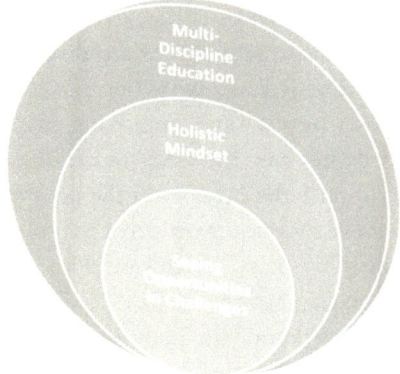

Discussion

Barriers to the Poor Learning Cycle

Poverty is a major cause of children not completing their learning, even if they manage to reach educational schemes or attend any school approaches mentioned. In India and similar to many developing and emerging economies countries, the gap in primary school completion rates between the richest and poorest children is more than 30%. A child's village or poverty area condition besides gender, family stability status, health, ethnic and cultural conditions, besides the economic background play a significant role in poor student learning cycle. Without real learning, any underprivileged child will not be able to succeed to go out of his/her trap (Buheji, 2019a; Suneja, 2015, Business Today, 2009).

Importance of Lifelong Learning Skills to Poverty Elimination

Poverty eradication through lifelong learning skills education is crucial for children of families that live under, or just above the poverty line. Current approaches are doing a great job to help India's government coop with the SDGs goals relevant to both eliminating poverty and improving literacy. However, these approaches do not have the seeds for lifelong learning skills that would help to raise the capacity of the poor for any sudden economic, or socio-economic downturn or natural crisis, like loss of jobs, or decline of business; which would lead to getting back to poverty situation trap again.

The formal education of the poor, often does not help the poor to break the poverty cycle. Teaching the poor to read and write, actually, make them learn more on how to care for their family and how to manage their life essentials, but does not equip them to explore other future opportunities. Developing programs as Akshar approach would help the poor to accumulate lifelong learning skills that would give them the capacity to avoid poverty-related practices and to empower themselves and their family, Khwaja (n.d.).

If people in high poverty areas are educated as lifelong learners, they will be able to climb out of poverty. Being lifelong learners would help the underprivileged students to see their choices and would give them the ability to improve themselves and their surrounding society. Buheji (2019d).

Lifelong learning would make the youth care more curious about the resources around them, and this means they would care more about the managing time and improve the way household are financed. Buheji (2019b).

Learning by Doing in Poverty Education

India's current educational poverty elimination approaches do not practice any 'Learning by doing' practices. 'Learning by doing', 'learning by exploring' and 'learning by trial', found to enhance the students' chances to live a curious life and thus enhance their capacity to achieve despite the limited resources (Buheji, 2019b).

'Learning by doing' empower the poor youth mental capacity and minimise their disability in dealing with 'life challenges'. Thus, the poor need to do projects to explore their available and hidden opportunities. Basically, 'learning by experimentation' will trigger a change in the mindset of the poor student. For instance, a person who has the right education might start a business at his community that will employ a few more people. The efforts of few will have an impact on the many.

Self-Sufficiency Education & its Importance to the Poor

The observations collected on poverty elimination education approaches do not carry any self-sufficiency skills that would help to raise their capacity in managing income-generating opportunities. With self-sufficiency based education and training, we could enable the poor children and youth to earn independence and see their capability to provide resources for their family, while they are studying. In addition to just earning, with self-sufficiency education, we can build in the mindset of the poor student also get aspiration and clarity for 'life-purposefulness' that would make them more persistent in getting over their personal sufferings and raising their capacity to contribute for the development of the rest of the society. Buheji (2019c).

Self-Sufficiency builds a sense of worth and helps to create total eradication of poverty. Once the poor children have a sense of worth, they would get motivated to improve their education and develop self-confidence to pursue their dreams. Khwaja (n.d.).

With self-sufficiency, the poverty family youth could pursue a better way of life, and target to seek a dream about a job, and become more competent in dealing with risks as overcoming material deprivation. Once self-sufficiency is established, we would have the poor better accessibility to their land ownership, livelihood and cultural commitment. This would ensure community development and effective economic justice.

Benefits of 'Door-Step' Slums Schools

Slums schools as 'door-steps schools', or 'teaching on the wheel', or new schools peer to peer education model as Akshar; all open opportunities to receive better education, health care and dignity-based work. Such education might provide critical thinking, networking and making friends and contacts. This would help to better sharing of ideas and solutions, and thus creating better self-driven solutions to fight poverty. Such schools help to build social integration, which helps knowledge sharing. Such students can be constructive to manage community meetings to improve living standards.

Education as a means for Appreciating the Wealth Assets

Wealth creation should be of a significant aspect in education programmes intended to contribute to poverty eradication. Education assists us in identifying the opportunities of the assets visible or invisible. Integration of school education within the economic activities of a community is essential for the effective return of such educational services on the student lives and their families. For instance, in a carpet-weaving village, lessons should also cover various aspects of the carpet industry. In this way, school education would help children to improve traditional trade skills of the village alongside other curricular contents. It would ensure their future employment possibilities and contribute to the (economic) wellbeing of the whole community. Furthermore, the school would not then be alienated from the community, and traditional trades would reinforce learning (Buheji, 2019a; Khwaja (n.d.)).

For the education system to truly respond to the needs of poor children and to contribute to wealth creation in communities and society at large, it needs to take the issue of poverty into special consideration in the planning of educational services. Essentially, it has to prepare the children to exploit their wealth and heighten the capacity of their rights and responsibilities and enhance their self-confidence to enable them to improve their lives. This means stocktaking of the assets of poor children and their families (a situation, conditions, reasons for poverty, etc.) so that appropriate support can be planned and targeted to them (Buheji, 2019a).

Conclusion and Recommendation

Enhancing India's Efforts in Eliminating Poverty through Education

India's population in poverty declined to reach below 25%; the effective elimination of poverty through education is becoming more and more difficult. Many underprivileged Indians are increasingly reaching educational access, however still and most probably be at a socio-economic disadvantage. Therefore, this research focus on improving the educational approaches for the poorest children in India, based on the collected field observations. The target of this work is to set a new line of research about the better mapping of educational access for children in poverty, specifically those in the rural areas and the slums of India.

Transforming Poverty Education towards Capacity vs Demand

Education supposed to build communication channels that lead the poor child or youth to express their own ideas and have the capacity to create change in their socio-economic status, or solve current or future challenges. To break the poverty cycle, poverty education should help to cater to children's diverse needs and even to provide additional support outside academic classes.

Therefore, a framework is suggested to the enhance the current approaches and transform their goals from being services that work just to fill the gap of India to meet the SDG, i.e. playing the role of 'Supply vs Demand', to approaches that work on the formula of 'Capacity vs Demand'. The proposed new formula of 'Capacity vs Demand' would focus on developing programs and schemes that establish a mindset that realises 'lifelong learning' skills, support 'learning by doing' practices, build self-sufficiency behaviours and lead to an appreciation of the wealth of assets available in the underprivileged.

Figure (8) Illustrate the importance of transforming the Educational poverty elimination approaches towards 'Capacity vs Demand'

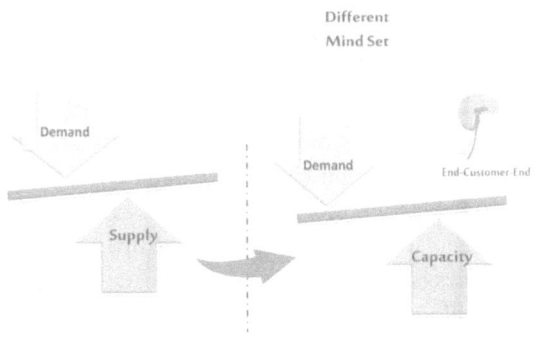

Through such proposed transformation, poverty elimination education approaches, India can do change management in the mindset of the future coming generation. This means establishing more holistic poverty elimination educational services that would ensure effective socio-economic change.

References

Buheji, M. (2018). *Re-Inventing Our Lives, A Handbook for Socio-Economic "Problem-Solving"*. AuthorHouse, UK.

Buheji, M. (2019a). 'Re-designing the Economic Discovery of Wealth' a Framework for Dealing with the Issue of Poverty. *International Journal of Economics, Commerce and Management, United Kingdom, Vol. VII, Issue 2, February.*, 387-398.

Buheji, M. (2019b). *Designing a Curious Life*. AuthorHouse, UK.

Buheji, M. (2019c). Poverty Labs-From 'Alleviation' to 'Elimination and then Prevention'. *Journal of Social Science Studies, 6(2)*, 108-122.

Buheji, M. (2019d). Shaping Future Type of Poverty-The Foresight of Future Socio-economic Problems & Solutions-Taking Poverty as a Context-Beyond 2030. *American Journal of Economics, 9(3)*, 106-117.

Business Today. (2009). *How to end poverty in India,*. Retrieved May 1, 2019, from https://www.businesstoday.in/magazine/special/how-to-end-poverty-in-india/story/4055.html

Education, G. P. (2016). *5 ways education can help end extreme poverty*. Retrieved from https://www.globalpartnership.org/blog/5-ways-education-can-help-end-extreme-poverty

GlobalPartnershipforEducation. (2019). *Education Data*. Retrieved from globalpartnership: https://www.globalpartnership.org/data-and-results/education-data

Hinteregger, T. (n.d.). *Poverty Rate in India*. Retrieved from https://borgenproject.org/poverty-rate-in-india-2/

Khwaja, M. (n.d.). *Education Alone cannot eradicate poverty, Fair Observer*. Retrieved from https://www.fairobserver.com/360_analysis/education-alone-cannot-eradicate-poverty-23320/

Kulild, V. (2014). *Role of education in ending extreme poverty- Taking a global lead, Norad, Carita seminar on the United Nations Sustainable Development Goals, Post-2015 Development Agenda, Oslo, 11th November*. Retrieved May 1, 2019, from https://norad.no/en/front/about-norad/news/role-of-education-in-ending-extreme-poverty--taking-a-global-lead/

Opportunity., E. C. (n.d.). *The Learning Generation, Investing in Education for a changing world – Executive Summary*. Retrieved from www.educationcommission.org

Payne, R. (2005). *A framework for understanding poverty (4th edition)*. Highland, TX: aha! Process, Inc.

SavetheChildren. (2017). *Eradication of poverty through education in India*. Retrieved from Save the Children: https://www.savethechildren.in/articles/eradication-of-poverty-through-education-in-india

Suneja, V. (2015). *Why ending poverty in India means tackling rural poverty and power*. Retrieved May 1, 2019, from https://www.oxfamindia.org/featuredstories/why-ending-poverty-india-means-tackling-rural-poverty-and-power

UNESCO. (2015). *EFA Global Monitoring, Reaching the marginalized Reaching the marginalized*. Retrieved from Education for All: https://unesdoc.unesco.org/ark:/48223/pf0000186606

UNESCO. (2015). *EFA Global Monitoring, United Nations Educational, Scientific and Cultural Organization.* Retrieved from EDUCATION FOR ALL 2000-2015: Achievements and Challenges, EFA Global Monitoring Report.

UNESCO. (2016). *EFA Global Monitoring, Education for All, United Nations Educational, Scientific and Cultural Organization.* Retrieved from TEACHING AND LEARNING: Achieving quality for all.: https://unesdoc.unesco.org/ark:/48223/pf0000225660

CHAPTER FIVE

Reviewing-Entrepreneurial Neighbourhoods: Towards an Understanding of the Economies of Neighbourhoods and Communities[5]

Introduction

This chapter review a book related to the issue of poverty, the book selectively and brilliantly integrates between entrepreneurship and neighbourhoods or communities. It sheds light about the importance of neighbourhood entrepreneurship to the socio-economic outcomes compared to other classical, technology-driven and youth-related entrepreneurship programs.

---

[5] Buheji, M (2018), Book Review-Entrepreneurial Neighbourhoods, Towards an Understanding of the Economies of Neighbourhoods and Communities, Journal of Social Science Studies, 5 (2), pp. 207-209.

Effects of Neighbourhood Entrepreneurs

Neighbourhood entrepreneurs (NE's) typically fall under the category of microbusinesses or sometimes called as micro-start businesses where they would have low initial capital with less than five employees. However, these microbusinesses contribute to 31% of the total employment of all private sector employment nationwide. The effects of microbusinesses are amplified and of particular relevance to low-income neighbourhoods. The influence of NE's goes beyond financial returns or the capitals employed; it actually causes social stability, community engagement, enhance society trust and most of all increase individuals and organisations resilience (Buheji, 2018).

Challenges of Low-Income Neighbourhoods

Entrepreneurs in low-income and minority neighbourhoods encounter numerous problems in securing their capital needs. However, the discussion today is more about program-related investments. Lack of capital is consistently cited as one of the top reasons leading to business failure. However, accessing capital in distressed neighbourhoods, particularly by small communities, is very challenging.

Given the entrepreneurial neighbourhood's lack of access to traditional sources of capital, there may be benefit from non-traditional sources, including private and institutional venture capital investors funding "neighbourhood" entrepreneurs.

The nonfinancial motives of venture capital decisions motives include a willingness to accept a lower return in order to support local economic development and minority entrepreneurs. Entrepreneurial neighbourhoods even though might be weaker in professional networking they are very strong in informal networks. However, neighbourhood entrepreneurs do not have the capacity to connect with investors.

Role of Entrepreneurial Neighbourhoods in Future

Future foresight sees that the new generation of businesses success would depend on how much it manages to deliver unique care to its customers. Entrepreneurial neighbourhoods would have higher equality in working with people regardless of their race, age, colour, religion and ethnicity. Entrepreneurial neighbourhoods also help immigrants and non-residents to develop their businesses allowing potential entrepreneurs to formalise their businesses and goals.

Entrepreneurial Neighbourhoods Creativity

Entrepreneurial neighbourhoods need more than ever today creativity to help the beneficiaries capture opportunities of the many localised spaces that build a collaborative sharing economy. Living labs help neighbourhood entrepreneurs to be more focused, open, collaborative and knowledge sharing (Buheji and Ahmed, 2017).

The work of van Ham et al. (2017) and his team represent many best practices in entrepreneurial neighbourhoods from UK, Holland and USA, including states as Detroit. As a reviewer, one could see the book missed a great opportunity of studying the influence of emerging economies neighbourhoods.

Neighbourhoods as Economic Places

In order for neighbourhoods to generate benefits in low income and minority communities, new ventures need to overcome the problem of limited access to capital and effectively spread risk between the entrepreneurs and the funding entities. However, this means that each neighbourhood is expected to build on its legal, financial and non-financial resources and to contribute to its community entrepreneurial efforts.

Conclusion

Entrepreneurial neighbourhoods' is a multi-disciplinary economic cluster book that helps to build a collective entrepreneurial spirit through entrepreneurship planning, urban planning, housing studies, economical studies and sociology.

The book calls for opportunities that cities and communities could use as a new niche as the economy increasingly rewards knowledge, innovation, and entrepreneurship. However, the authors transparently admit that despite such programs, many neighbourhoods still face the troubling legacy of persistent poverty and racial separation as well as the continued decentralisation of economic and residential life.

Due to having many economies in the transition while having an ageing population, entrepreneurial neighbourhoods are of high importance. van Ham et al. (2017) work challenge us to see even the economic relevance of urban policies and how it addresses communities and cities needs and demands. Achieving this objective will not only improve the condition of cities, but it would even substantially improve the whole national economy.

Due to consistent demographic changes, diverse approaches are needed to address the entrepreneurial needs. The book calls for a total review for the way education, training, wages, financial services, health care, and housing services are delivered, and it should be in order to build the future entrepreneurial neighbourhood. The authors of this book managed to illustrate more life opportunities that show the role of urban residents for both local and national economy.

This book is highly recommended for postgraduates studying entrepreneurship, innovation, creativity, social psychology, behavioural economics, community urban planning engineering and change management. It a very suitable book for those who work on spreading non-classical economics and work in foresight a better socio-economic future and strive for it.

References

Buheji, M (2018) Understanding the Power of Resilience Economy: An Inter-Disciplinary Perspective to Change the World Attitude to Socio-Economic Crisis, AuthorHouse, UK.

Buheji, M and Ahmed, D (2017) Review Paper-Creative Destruction and the Sharing Economy, International Journal of Youth Economy, Vol 1, Issue 1, March, pp. 119-120,

Brewer, J and Gibson, S (2016) Institutional Case Studies On Necessity Entrepreneurship. Edward Elgar, UK

CHAPTER SIX

Discovering Pathways for Eliminating NEET and Youth Future Type of Poverty[6]

Abstract

When youth and NEET are mentioned together you do not only remember 'youth not in employment, not in education, or not in training', but it would also evoke your mind that it is a new type of poverty. Therefore, this paper explores the different possibilities and alternatives of dealing with NEET youth cases either before, or during, or after NEET issues occur and how to keep them away from filling into the new poverty trap.

The paper reviews the International Inspiration Economy Project (IIEP) approaches in eliminating possibilities of poverty in relevance to NEET youth. Forty case projects are presented and categorised into three types of 'intrinsic capacity' practices that could be established to prevent or treat NEET youth. The framework proposes creating a new wave of thinking on the management of NEET to avoid a sophisticated type of poverty.

---

[6] Buheji, M (2019) Discovering Pathways for Eliminating NEET and Youth Future Type of Poverty, International Journal of Human Resource Studies, Vol. 9, No. 3, August, pp. 320-340.

The common thread of all solutions proposed is the optimisation of 'visualisation techniques' which could be established in the life of youth and used to raise their capacity towards eliminating the possibilities of falling into any type of poverty.

Keyword: NEET, Poverty Elimination, Youth Economy, Youth Future Poverty, Inspiration Economy Projects.

Introduction

NEET of youth; i.e. youth not in employment, or education, or training has been rising as a subject in literature in the last one decade, especially with the emphasis of international agencies reports that are trying to address the issues of millennium-and then sustainable-development goals (MDGs and SDGs) in relevance to youth empowerment and poverty elimination.

The term NEET was first used in the UK and then started to spread in developed countries as the USA and Japan. In the United Kingdom, the classification of NEET comprises people aged between 16 and 24. The subgroup of NEETs aged 16–18 is frequently of particular focus. In Japan, the classification comprises people aged between 15 and 34 who are not employed, not engaged in housework, not enrolled in schoolو or work-related training and not seeking promised work. Eurofound (2012)

A 2008 report by the OECD said the unemployment of NEET rates for people aged 16–24 in the majority of OECD countries fell in the past decade, attributed to increased participation in education. The OECD put NEET as a percentage of the total number of young people in the corresponding age group, by gender. Young people in education include those attending part-time or full-time education, but exclude those in non-formal education and educational activities of very short duration. Employment is defined according to the OECD/ILO Guidelines and covers all those who have been in paid work for at least one hour in the reference week of the survey or were temporarily absent from such work. Therefore, NEET youth can be either unemployed or inactive and not involved in education or training. Young people who are neither in employment nor in education or training are at risk of becoming socially excluded. Many of these NEET are, in reality, individuals live with income below the poverty-line and lacking the skills to improve their economic situation. Elder (2015), Eurofound (2012), ILO (2012).

This paper reviews different definitions of issue of NEET, which are reflected on its measured variables. The researcher presents the current categorising of NEET and the type of efforts in gauging its influence on governments and communities' performance.

Variety of NEET impact are presented, and then the different NEETs diagnosis and intervention programs are synthesised from the reviewed literature. This is followed by prevention programs in relevance to NEETs and the poverty that comes as a result of its availability. The alternative options of self-sufficiency and other programs that lead to better stable communities are listed. Other challenges of NEET in entering the labour market, or what leads to social exclusion are listed out. Good Practices in dealing with NEET and current NEET elimination or symptoms alleviation are summarised at the end of this review. Buheji (2018b), Newton and Buzzeo (2015), Prince Trust (2007).

Literature Review

Defining and Measuring NEET

Since there is no international standard for the definition of NEETs. This in itself could hinder the job of international advisers to countries on the new SDGs.

The best definition of NEET is the Eurostat and the ILO definition which both defined NEET rate as the percentage of the population of a given age group and sex who are not employed and not involved in further education or training. The numerator of the indicator refers to persons meeting two conditions: (i) they are not employed (i.e. are unemployed or inactive), and (ii) they have not received any education or training in the four weeks preceding the survey. The denominator, according to Eurostat, is the total population of the same age and sex group, excluding respondents who have not answered the question "Participation to regular education and training". Elder (2015).

The newly coined NLFET rate "neither in the labour force nor in education or training" used in the 2013 report on Global Employment Trends for Youth by the International Labor Organisation (ILO). It is similar to NEET, but it excludes the unemployed youth (who are part of the labour force). Furlong (2006), ILO (2012).

The ILO (2013) has put the following NEET rate (%) = (Number of youth – number of youth in employment + number of youth not in employment who are in education or training) x 100. The total number of youth formula: unemployed non-students + inactive non-students' in relevance to youth population. Elder (2015), ILO (2012).

Current literature frequently simplifies the measurement of NEETs to unemployed + inactive non-students, ignoring the fact that some unemployed persons are also students and should thus be excluded from the calculation. (Hussmanns et al., 1990). The problem that if a student worked for at least one hour in the reference week, he or she is thus counted among the employed. If a student did not work, was available to work and actively sought work, he or she is counted among the unemployed. Figure (1) illustrates the results of the calculated NEET rates. ILO (2012)

The Intent

Figure (1) Shows the NEET rates in selected countries

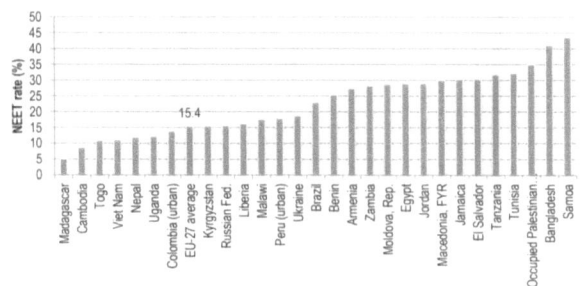

Sources: Hussmanns et. al. (1990) and ILO (2017) school-to-work transition survey.
http://www.ilo.org/employment/areas/WCMS_234860/lang--en/index.htm.

A detailed analysis of the subcategories of NEETs shows that it is made from the predominantly percentage of unemployed non-students and the non-active students. Most of the developing countries found to have a NEET rate of 28%, as shown in Figure (2).

Figure (2) Youth NEET rate and composition, selected countries statistics in 2012

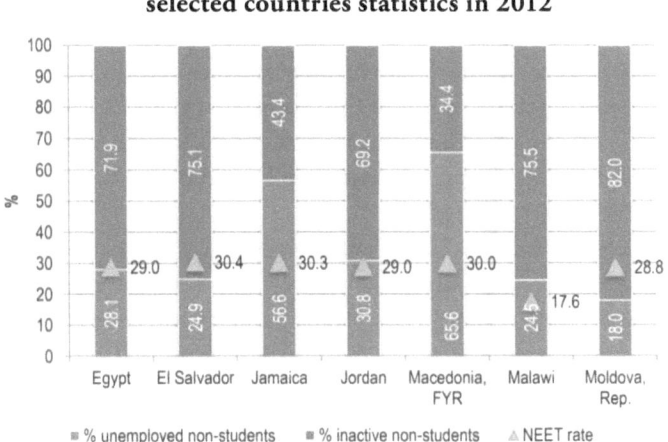

Source: Hussmanns et. al. (1990) and ILO school-to-work transition surveys
http://www.ilo.org/employment/areas/WCMS_234860/lang–en/index.htm.

Categorising NEET

Technically, NEET status and joblessness the same. The first subcategory of the NEETs is those "not in employment", i.e. the jobless. However, the "not in education or training" (inactive non-students) are also included as NEETs. To equate these inactive youths with the jobless would be erroneous. Again, technically, yes, they are without a job, but according to the international standards, this group has indicated that they did not actively seek work or they were not available to take up work. One cannot assume that it is their goal to have a job. The majority in this category in almost all countries are young women tending to the household. Robson (2010).

Categorising NEETs has come increasingly important and complicated. NEET issue and statistics are now a current and a future foresight issue with many changes in the socio-economic dynamics, including the fast development of Artificial Intelligence (AI) which is going to eliminate or change many jobs. Therefore, NEET is becoming the interest of the decision-makers in all the sector: governments, international organisations, research institutions and the media.

As an indicator, NEET has developed a lot to be now more precise for measuring the type of early school leavers, the unemployed youth and those youths out of the support and motivation system. NEET has become a label that grouping vulnerable youth. In certain countries, NEET indicator even includes those youths that are being labelled as family carers,

The Intent

or chronically sick, or not functional due to disability. Furlong (2006).

Realising NEET Impact

NEET impact varies from country to country. For example, the impact of NEET in 13 European countries for youth in ages of 15 to 29 years olds is higher than 25%. This rate might come upper or lower by 10%, as per Eurofound (2012).

To realise the impact of the NEETs, just imagine what an unemployed, vulnerable youth would do, or what possibilities they would be reckless or astray, or see their important role in the society. Studies the risk of losing the NEET energy and spirit and the loosing opportunities of the economy they could be generated from youth are increasing rapidly due the significant number and length of time these youths stay in this category, Buheji (2018). Studies now show that NEET is substantially increasing in ages 20–24, which is the age of best productivity and learning. NEETs get even more complicated in ages of 25 and 29. Kraus (2008).

Studies shows that young women today and the near future are at higher risks of becoming NEETs than young men in almost all countries. This would impact the family stability and the claimed gender equality. Robson (2010).

It is clear now there is high a relation between the type of education and its way in dealing with current and the future foresight of the labour market and issue of NEETs in any country. Studies now confirm that education might increase the risk of being NEET in some countries, while decreasing those NEET rates in others. Furlong (2006).

The socio-economic characteristics of youth, the type of youth culture or community, the family status, requires a specific capacity from the NEET to mitigate their risk from going into further economic difficulties. For example, if the NEET comes from an immigrant family, or from low income one, or unemployed parents, there might be a high risk that these youths would be marginalised, due to their skills, language, or simply to being from a specific minority. Furthermore, youth might suffer more exclusion from specific empowerment services that get them out NEET status for variety of reasons, which in the end increase their vulnerability. Today there are increasing worries that number of countries who losing control of this increase of youth vulnerability are becoming more a majority. This is establishing a clear bridge between the status of being NEET youth and youth in poverty. Buheji (2018), Prince Trust (2007), Furlong (2006).

3.4 NEET and Youth Poverty Elimination

In order to eliminate any potential new future type of youth poverty, governments are highly expected to provide specific guaranteed quality of life services as the right to education and skills development, the right for housing, the right for childcare support, the right for a suitable primary, secondary or apprenticeship education; beside the right for healthcare and transport.

Part of the proposed techniques to eliminate any possibility of youth poverty in NEET is to put more efforts on youth with trapped in inferior jobs or any type of status that make youth 'inactive'. The other type of eliminating future youth poverty in NEET is to keep categorising and developing the different potential vulnerable youth under one heading and then pre-test the designs targeted to address the challenges NEET face.

Today across the OECD, 22% of working-age adults under 30, and 18% of those over 30, would be below the poverty line if they did not receive benefits. However, income support is less effective

The Intent

in keeping youth out of poverty in the long run. OECD (2016). In emerging and developing countries, 16 to 20 per cent of young workers lives on income below the threshold of extreme-poverty, i.e. US$1.90 a day, partly because they often start their working lives in the informal economy. Newton and Buzzeo (2015).

Young people face a greater risk of poverty than older age groups. Young people are now more likely to be poor than seniors. Studies show that youth poverty rates are higher than seniors' rates in most OECD countries. Roughly every eighth young person lives in poverty OECD-wide. Youth poverty rates are particularly high in the Nordic countries, where young people tend to move out, so no longer benefit from their parents' income, earlier than in other countries. They are high in the USA too, although the population is somewhat younger. This increases much more in the absence of adequate public support; declining household incomes increase the risk of poverty. Time (2016).

NEETs Diagnosis and intervention programs

Diagnosis of socio-economic define its ways of intervention. Due to the magnitude and speed of the rising NEET problem, the interventions of NEETs, are still slow to in exploiting its underlying causes. Some the diagnosis takes us to the causes that come from the youth individual characteristics as their sex, education level, age, socio-economic background. Others believe that family or the community play an important factor in NEET.

The world needs more serious efforts in determining the dilemma that occurs when the intention is to create the youth transitions from education to employment, Brinton (2011). More studies need to see what type of social norms, or structures of education or vocational education and training (VET) need to ensure no more repeated NEET cases dumped on the governments burden. Shepherd (2011).

The amount of income support available to low-income young people, does not prevent them from being poor. As a consequence of the difficult labour market situation for young people is that a growing share of them struggle to be self-sufficient. Although income support can help absorb severe earnings losses and ensure a decent standard of living, it is often less generous and more difficult to access for young people. Shepherd (2011).

Studies show there are limited youth income support programs which they receive unemployment or disability benefits, social assistance, or other types of cash benefits, compared to adults. Yates and Payne (2006).

In EU and many leading developed countries where a high proportion of NEETs do not live with their parents, they may be at a higher risk of poverty, particularly if they live alone or in a household where nobody earns an income. Roughly every eighth young person lives in poverty OECD-wide, Time (2016). Youth poverty rates are particularly high in the Nordic countries, where the young tend to move out, so no longer benefit from their parents' income, earlier than in other countries. While income support is essential in the fight against youth poverty by itself, it is seldom enough to put young people back on the path to self-sufficiency. The best way to achieve lasting financial security is to secure stable employment. Robson (2010).

While the long-term goal of public policies is to help young people on the path to self-sufficiency, those on low incomes, especially the NEETs, may require support to avoid poverty. One way to achieve both objectives is to tie income support payments to young people's efforts to find a job or upskill. Benefits should allow young people to meet their basic needs, so they stay healthy and do not withdraw from society. In that regard, income support programmes have played an important role to protect the most vulnerable groups in the recent crisis and its aftermath. Shepherd (2011).

The Intent

NEETs Prevention Efforts

Many countries are taking serious efforts to modernise secondary education with vocational education and training opportunities. Emerging economies need to be able to create enough skilled jobs with less-educated young people.

Tackling information gaps for these unprotected groups is the first step in developing appropriate and targeted policy interventions. Among many different policy options, partner countries need to prioritise the prevention of early school leaving, the modernisation of secondary education, besides the integration of young women into education. Cox (2006).

In order to break the cycle of social exclusion of NEETs among youth more qualitative, effective, labour market-relevant and balanced education and training systems need to be developed, Prince Trust (2007). A participatory and coordinated action plan involving families, early child educators, schools (especially secondary and vocational schools), training providers, public employment services, youth organisations and the private sector is needed to ensure early tracking of disengagement and prompt intervention. There is some evidence that intensive multi-component interventions effectively decrease unemployment amongst NEETs. Kraus (2008).

The prevention program needs to focus on the 'discouraged youth' who have given up on job searching for reasons that imply a sense of despair about the labour market. In statistical terms, discouraged youth are without work and available to work but did not seek work for one of the following reasons: not knowing how or where to seek work; an inability to find work matching their skills; previous job searches had led to no results; feeling too young to find work; and the sense that no jobs were available in the area. Given the frequency with which the term "discouraged youth", also called sometimes as the "lost generation" has been used to draw attention to youth issues throughout the economic crisis and subsequent great recession. Among the NEETs, 'discouraged youth' made up 10% of the total, on average.

One of the challenges of NEETs poverty is poor health. Studies show that about 7%-10% of youth on average across the OECD countries report being in poor health to the extent which limits their daily activity. In developing and underdeveloped countries, NEET youth with poor health might increase from 30%-40%. Hussmanns et al. (1990).

Communities Stabilities and the Challenge of NEET

Youth comprise 40% of the world's unemployed, a status associated with adverse wellbeing and social, health, and economic costs. This systematic review and meta-analysis review synthesises the literature on the effectiveness of interventions targeting young people, not in employment, education, or training (NEET).

In 2017, 16.7 per cent of working youth in emerging and developing countries living below the extreme poverty threshold of US$1.90 per day. y The bulk of international migrant flows consists of young people – around 70 per cent are younger than 30. y Between now and 2030, the global youth labour force will expand by 25.6 million, driven by trends in Africa; these young people will need jobs. Hussmanns et al. (1990).

In 2017, the youth continued to fare worse than adults – approximately 28 per cent of young workers are poor, compared with about 19 per cent of adults. That young worker is more likely to be in working poverty than adults in virtually all regions is connected to the higher incidence of young workers in the informal economy, notably in developing and emerging countries. Globally, more than three-quarters (76.7 per cent) of working youth are in informal jobs. Newton and Buzzeo (2015).

The Intent

The youth NEET rate of the EU-27 countries was 15.4 per cent in 2012 (Eurofound, 2012). Is this the NEET rate to aim for? Again, without additional information, we are unable to prescribe an acceptable youth NEET rate. The picture is further skewed when we note in Figure 2 that the average youth NEET rate in low-income countries was nearly on par with that of the high-income countries (18.1 and 15.5 per cent, respectively). It is in the middle-income countries that countries have the greatest difficulty in keeping the youth population fully engaged. Kraus (2008).

Young adults who are not in employment, education and training (NEET) are at risk of becoming socially excluded with income below the poverty line and lacking the skills to improve their economic situation (Carcillo et al., 2015) as shown in Figure (3). Newton and Buzzeo (2015).

Figure (3) Youth NEET rate for (2012/2013) by type of income and regional groupings.

Grouping	NEET rate (%)
Low-income	18.1
Lower middle-income	26.8
Upper middle-income	25.2
High-income	15.5
Asia & Pacific	23.3
Eastern Europe & Central Asia	24.1
Latin America & Caribbean	23.1
Middle East & North Africa	31.3
Sub-Saharan Africa	18.4

Sources: Hussmanns et al. (1990) calculations based on ILO school-to-work transition surveys (www.ilo.org/w4y) and Eurofound (2012) for EU-27.

Mohamed Buheji & Dunya Ahmed

The Challenge of NEET in Labor Market

Young people today struggle in the labour market despite being the most highly educated generation in history. Unemployment is generally higher among young people than prime-age adults, and those who do work tend to have poorer-quality jobs and are much more likely to be on temporary contracts or to earn low wages than older workers.

With limited options for educational attainment and lack of social safety nets, most youths in low-income countries are engaged in some form of income-generating activity. Employment is the only option for most youth in poor countries. Yet the quality of available employment offers little scope for youth to gain a stable, prosperous livelihood. Without a qualitative employment indicator, we will never gain proper insight into the labour market challenges faced by the majority of the world's youth population. Yates and Payne (2006).

The OECD revealed that there are more than 580,000 young Australians between the ages of 15 and 29 fall under the classification of NEET. Many countries have been having an increase in NEET since the global financial crisis. A survey about NEETs in Canada in 2012 revealed that around 13% of Canadians between the ages of 15 and 29 fell into the category. The study revealed that out of the total 904,000 NEETs around 513,000 were not looking actively for jobs, and then many of the rest of NEETs are not contracted based on long-term employment. Robson (2010).

In Latin American and the Caribbean, the World Bank estimates one in five people ages 15–24 are NEETs, 20 million in total and which two-thirds are women. In Mexico, at least a quarter of youth are classified as NEET and are highly correlated with increased homicides in high-crime. In the USA at 15% are classified as NEETs and are called as "marginalized group of young people". While in Korea, NEET is considered even those who do not even complete high school education. Time (2016).

NEET and Social Exclusion

NEET as a word spread after it was used in a 1999 report by the social exclusion unit. Before this, the phrase "status zero", which had a similar meaning, was used. Andy Furlong writes that the use of the term NEET became popular partly because of the negative connotations of having "no status" in society. The classification is specifically redefined as "respondents who were out of work or looking for a job, looking after children or family members, on unpaid holiday or travelling, sick or disabled, doing voluntary work or engaged in another unspecified activity". However, despite many NEET definitions, there is no original measurement attempt in relevance to influence on economic inactivity. Prince Trust (2007).

Scott Yates and Malcolm Payne say that initially there was a "holistic focus" on the NEET group by policy-makers which looked at the problems young people went through, but this changed as the NEET status became framed in negative terms—"as reflective of a raft of risks, problems and negative orientations on the part of young people".

Good Practices in dealing with NEET

One of the NEET figures for England is published by the Department of Education (DfE). The methodology used in calculating the number of NEETs aged 16–18 is different from that used for those aged 16–24. The first relies on a range of sources, the second on the Labour Market Surveys.

A 2007 report commissioned by the Prince's Trust said almost a fifth of people aged 16–24 in the UK were NEETs. *The Guardian (2011)* report that, since 2003, there has been a 15.6 per cent decrease in people aged 16–18 in employment, but a 6.8 per cent increase in those in education and training. NEET figures tend to peak in the third quarter, when school and university courses are ending.

There is some stigma attached to the term NEET. Simon Cox of BBC News said the word is "the latest buzzword for teenage drop-outs". He says "NEETs are 20 times more likely to commit a crime and 22 times more likely to be a teenage mum".

NEET if tackled from different perspectives as educational, social, and psychological resources, could help youth to enter and maintaining education or employment. However, by the perspective of life span developmental psychology, this places particular pressure on those young people growing up in disadvantaged circumstances and lacking support, especially when attempting to negotiate the transition from school to work. Brinton (2011).

Schemes of NEET

Several schemes and ideas have been developed to reduce the number of NEETs. UK government, for example, introduced an allowance of £30 to young people continuing education past secondary school. Then, "Young Person's Guarantee" scheme was announced guaranteed suitable learning place for the 16-year-old school leavers in 2009, offering a guaranteed job, training, or work experience to 18-to 24-year-olds. The agreement helps the colleges to seek to enrol NEETs. Kraus (2008).

Japanese government expressed concern about the impact on the economy of the growth in the NEET population. According to the Japanese Ministry of Health, Labor and Welfare. Other surveys by the Japanese government in 2002 presented a much larger figure of 850,000 people who can be classified as NEET, of which 60% were people aged 25 to 34. When the NEET issue erupted in the Japanese media in 2004 and 2005, non-employed young people falling into this category were framed as lazy, work-shy and voluntarily out of employment. This media portrayal was effective in arousing the concern of Japan's (conservative) middle-aged population, but it led only to moderate support for new youth policies.

Many NEETs in Japan use 'Youth Support Stations' services, which are designed by social enterprises, to support youth. Some believe that Japanese NEETs include many who have rejected the accepted social model of adulthood. They are said to not actively seek full-time employment after graduation, or further training to obtain marketable job skills through the governmental 'hello work' schemes.

Professor Michiko Miyamoto describes the situation as a "breakdown of the social framework forged in an industrial society, by which young people become adults."

Methodology

The research methodology employed in this paper uses a qualitative case study approach. The case study is a collection of 40 projects cases that were chosen from a longitudinal research study conducted by the International Inspiration Economy Project (IIEP). The method used the target to help explore the possibilities in dealing with NEET complex and multiple variables, practices and processes (Yin, 2003).

The study examined three types of projects cases that prevent, treat or improve the techniques related to NEETs in relevance to the targeted groups which are usually youth between the age of 13-32, where they should be in schools or universities, or working as part-time — the projects listed help to develop the 'intrinsic capacities' in relevance to the type of challenges. The 'intrinsic capacities' are extracted from the longitudinal study cases and projects. Besides, the types of projects, each case was categorised into one three targeted practices that help to develop the youth 'intrinsic capacity' and keep them protected from failing into NEET or poverty traps: visualisation-driven practice, choices-driven practice, decision-driven practice. Buheji (2019), Eurofound (2012).

The case study and the 40 projects enable the investigation for a suitable framework that would build a full variety of evidence: documents, artefacts, interviews and observations. The paper attempts to address the research question: "How NEET can be eliminated or its influence reduced on youth in a way that it would not lead to a new type of poverty?"

Case Studies

Since September 2015 till September 2018 IIEP carried projects that deal with the issue of NEET youth from different perspectives and using a variety of approaches. The case studies were carried in mainly four countries, Bahrain, Bosnia, Mauritania and Morocco, over the three years. The motivation for such projects was IIEP carries in it themes the passion 'youth economy' and 'resilience economy', besides 'inspiration economy' which are highly related to both preventions of NEET side effects and elimination of poverty. Buheji (2018a, b, c).

For the sake of this research, the IIEP projects were categorised into mainly three types of cases. The first type of cases was focused on how to control the influence of NEET and its effect, including the negative influence and the possibility of poverty creation. The second type of categorised cases was focused on treating NEET youth to recover from poverty or poverty-related effects. The third type of cases is focused on improving the capacity of youth to help to be more resilient and not fail into the NEET trap, or to re-integrate these youths into the society, or eliminate possible exclusion, Buheji (2018c).

All the projects targeted to enhance youth 'intrinsic capacity' and keep them protected from failing into NEET or poverty traps by focusing on one of the following practices: visualisation-driven practice, choices-driven practice, decision-driven practice. Buheji (2019).

Type 1 Cases-Preventing NEET Trap or Possibility of Side Effects (including living with poverty symptoms).

In order to prevent students and youth generation from getting into the NEET trap and side effects; including living into poverty symptoms; the following cases were carried out in different times during the 9/2015 till 9/2018, as per the following Table (1). Each of the projects cases targeted a specific group of NEET during school life, before graduation or directly after graduation.

Table (1) Illustrate Projects that target to prevent NEET trap

Project Case	NEET Target Group	Countries Involved	'Intrinsic Capacity' Practice Targeted
1-Build a knowledge economy driven practices in selected schools and universities.	Students of both Schools & Universities	Bahrain	Choices of Life

Project Case	NEET Target Group	Countries Involved	'Intrinsic Capacity' Practice Targeted
2-Integrated extra-curricular programs in schools and universities with lifelong learning skills programs.	Students of both Schools & Universities	Bahrain, Bosnia	Visualisation /Choices of Life
3-Enhance multi-disciplinary approaches in the university curriculum as per the type of colleges speciality and disciplines.	Graduating Higher Education Students	Bahrain, Bosnia and Mauritania	Visualisation /Choices of Life
4-Develop 'elementary till university' students 'scientific and research contribution passion' and make them focus on developing their countries 'innovation index' by more focused projects that influence their choices in life.	All youth from 13-32 years old in and outside the education system	Bahrain (University of Bahrain) and (with some selected Bosnian Schools and Universities)	Visualisation /Choices of Life / Decision-Making
5-Use the power of peer-to-peer influence to improve 'non-performing students' and ensure these students meets	Non-Performing Students in all school ages of 13-19 years old	Bahrain, Bosnia, (With selected schools in Morocco and Mauritania)	Choices of Life

The Intent

Project Case	NEET Target Group	Countries Involved	'Intrinsic Capacity' Practice Targeted
the minimal standard of education.			
6-Support Spreading Classes and then Schools Self-Sufficiency Scheme Models	Elementary till High Schools	Bosnia Schools	Choices of Life
7-Simplify tools for measuring students' safety or positive psychology or stress release.	High School & University Students	Bahrain (University of Bahrain) and (with some selected Bosnian Schools and Universities)	Choices of Life
8-Improve the academic counselling that enhance the students' graduation time and give proper guidance at the right time.	High School & University Students	Bahrain (University of Bahrain)	Choices of Life
9-Spread the Disruptive Learning and flipped class teaching techniques to ensure suitable preparedness for the coming life challenges.	High School & University Students	Bahrain (University of Bahrain) and (with some selected Bosnian Schools and Universities)	Visualisation
9-Setting Seasonal life-purposefulness Programs that	Students of both Schools & Universities	Bahrain (University of Bahrain) and (with some	Visualisation

Project Case	NEET Target Group	Countries Involved	'Intrinsic Capacity' Practice Targeted
change the mindset of youth about their seen and hidden choices in life.		selected Bosnian Schools and Universities)	
11-Addressing the Gambling (pitting) behaviour amongst youth and building prevention scheme through schools' model	Students of both Schools & Universities	Bosnia High Schools	Visualisation Choices of Life
12-Sponsoring projects that analysis the codification and classification of the type of students challenges and problems as per the counselling services of social workers and students deanship.	NEET and Students from age 13-32	Bahrain (University of Bahrain) and (with some selected Bosnian Schools and Universities)	Visualisation /Choices of Life
13-Developing capacity of youth entrepreneurs to increase the survival of their start-ups for more than three years (on average), or the development of safe exits plans.	Youth Entrepreneurs	Bahrain, Morocco, Mauritania	Visualisation /Choices of Life / Decision-Making

The Intent

Type 2 Cases-Treating NEET to recover from Poverty

The second type of cases in IIEP is focused on treating NEET youth to recover from the potential of into poverty and poverty-related symptoms, which are reflected in Table (2). The treatment practices work on either easing the access of youth to sources of NEET prevention programs or mitigating the impact of negative influences that are leading or could lead to NEET status.

Table (2) Illustrate NEET or NEET prone cases and how they are treated from becoming or being in poverty.

Project Case	NEET Target Group	Countries Involved	'Intrinsic Capacity' Practice Targeted
1-Easing access to schools and reducing the tuitions specifically to encourage girls' education among the villagers.	Female Students of both Schools & Universities	Morocco, Mauritania	Visualisation /Choices of Life
2-Focus on finding alternatives for the girls' role in the village, i.e. easing water transport to release the girls for schools' attendance.	Female Students of both Schools & Universities	Morocco, Mauritania	Visualisation /Choices of Life
3-Show the benefit and the differentiation	Students of both Schools & Universities	Bosnia	Visualisation /Choices of Life

Project Case	NEET Target Group	Countries Involved	'Intrinsic Capacity' Practice Targeted
of the 'Non-Performing Students' towards the Society and the Socio-Economy.			
4-Establishing Dropout Students micro start companies	Students of both Schools & Universities	Bosnia and Mauritania	Visualisation /Choices of Life / Decision-Making
4-Reduce Migration of Youth with more employment opportunities for the villagers' families.	Youth believing in Migration as a goal from age 13-32	Bosnia and Morocco	Visualisation /Choices of Life / Decision-Making
5-Build a 'youth trust' in the village system as a source of income	Youth of Villagers Families	Villages of Morocco Mountains and Mauritania	Visualisation /Choices of Life
6-Build 'youth independence program' that counter the poverty through raising the capacity of the farmers for competitive packaging and distribution.	Youth of farmers families and communities	Bahrain, Morocco, Mauritania and Bosnia	Visualisation /Choices of Life / Decision-Making
7-Define type of expelling factors that NEET youth goes through in School, University,	Youth on the risk of being expelled or being NEET or being Excluded from their community	Bahrain	/Choices of Life

The Intent

Project Case	NEET Target Group	Countries Involved	'Intrinsic Capacity' Practice Targeted
NGOs, Private Sector, Friends or Family.			
8-Define and then tackle issues of students' depression and calculate its return on the society flourishment.	Cases of Students whom Seeking Council or Dropped in Performance	Bahrain and Bosnia	Choices of Life
9-Reduce youth suicide ratio due to early treatment of main causalities of NEET symptoms and none availability of clear life-purposefulness.	Youth who experience Anxiety	Bahrain and Bosnia	Visualisation /Choices of Life
10-Integrating NEET youth with both formal sport and traditional games to eliminate 'imposter syndrome'.	Youth on Risky Communities or from Drugs Areas	Bosnia	Visualisation /Choices of Life
11-Engaging troubled NEET youth in Police Patrols.	Troubled NEET Youth or Youth with history bad incidents	Bahrain	Visualisation /Choices of Life

Type 3 Cases-Improving the Capacity of youth to eliminate any type of NEET that causes poverty

The third type of cases in this study was focused on selecting IIEP projects that worked on improving the capacity of youth in order to prevent them from becoming unemployed, or get stuck with a job they are not passionate about, or lose opportunities that make them live as part of poverty, as per Table (3). Achieving such projects would make young people more resilient to meet the turbulent conditions of the labour market.

Table (3) Illustrates the projects that focused on raising the capacity of youth to eliminate any type of NEET related poverty.

Project Case	NEET Target Group	Countries Involved	'Intrinsic Capacity' Practice Targeted
1-Inspiring students to see their intrinsic powers, while developing their creative thinking skills	Students of both Schools & Universities	Bahrain, Bosnia, Morocco, Mauritania	Visualisation /Choices of Life
2-Discovering inspiring students at the right time. (Early inspiration discovery program).	Students of Schools	Bahrain	Visualisation
3-Establishing track of the inspired students after graduation (Inspiration Pathways).	Graduating High School or University Students	Bahrain	Visualisation /Choices of Life
4-Re-Inventing the influence effect of 'Students Volunteering Program'	Students of both Schools & Universities	Bahrain and Selected Mauritania NGOs youth	Visualisation /Choices of Life

The Intent

Project Case	NEET Target Group	Countries Involved	'Intrinsic Capacity' Practice Targeted
5-Improving academic counselling that enhance the students' graduation time and give proper guidance towards their proper life goals, in the right time.	Late graduating students or low performing students or part-time students Or NEET youth	Bahrain	Visualisation /Choices of Life /Decision-Making
6-Improve the University capability to attract competitive projects and contracts through re-organising its students' knowledge expertise and profile.	Students of both Schools & Universities	Bahrain	Visualisation /Choices of Life
7-Enhance students' fitness or competence to meet labour market demand through encouraging different jobs engagement before graduation.	High School and University Graduating Students	Bahrain	Visualisation /Choices of Life /Decision-Making
8-Optimise the Youth 'Quality of Life' through Students Unions Focused 'Pull thinking' Projects	All Youth with more focus on NEET	Bosnia	Visualisation /Choices of Life/Decision-Making
9-Building Youth Entrepreneurship & Innovation programs.	Graduating Youth	Bahrain and Bosnia	Visualisation /Choices of Life/Decision-Making
10-Enhancing Youth contribution in voluntary work through rectifying and supporting change in Cultural and Sports Clubs.	All youth from 13-32 years	Bahrain and Selected Mauritania NGOs youth	Visualisation /Choices of Life/Decision-Making

Project Case	NEET Target Group	Countries Involved	'Intrinsic Capacity' Practice Targeted
11-Enhancing Potential Employers engagement with schools, colleges and universities and improve the feedback Students interaction and readiness to challenges of the local economy.	Students of both Schools & Universities	Bahrain	Choices of Life/Decision-Making
14-Show influence of 'Disruptive Education' and 'Multi-discipline Learning' on creating more inspiring students.	Students of both Schools & Universities	Bahrain, Bosnia and Morocco	Visualisation /Choices of Life
15-Simulate experiments & hands-on to enhance the community innovation around the university campus.	Students of Universities	Bahrain	Visualisation /Choices of Life
16-Improving the outcome of creating "Self-Dependent" youth in the 'Police Youth Summer Camps' which is held for 3 weeks.	Youth between 11-16 years	Bahrain	Visualisation /Choices of Life

Discussion

Reviewing both literature and the rising challenges of NEET and NEET related outcomes shows there is still much work need to be done in this area specifically in relation raising the intrinsic capacities of youth either to overcome the trap of NEET

The Intent

or prevent them from being inside it. The three types of cases in relevance to preventing, treating or improving the youth to keep them away from NEET related problems or being trapped in NEET opens up a new line of research.

The IIEP program sets examples of how we could deal with NEET youth challenges, as the youth with no employment opportunities, or in those in unstable jobs, or in low paid jobs. Most of the three types of cases show the importance of visualisation and setting practices that enhance or calibrate or exploit life-purposefulness goals.

The case study helps to set a NEET transformation framework that helps to deal with the symptoms of youth, which lead to cases of stress, tension and then even might develop to chronic depression. The trend now for these NEET related symptoms come as 'quarter-life crisis', where NEET youth feel they have no clear life-purposefulness goals. Some NEETs also more might develop 'Imposter Syndrome', where youth would 'feel of none appreciation of their achievements'.

In order to raise excitement and minimise the NEET youth dissatisfaction, as per Figure (4), we need to develop for the techniques that increase their 'visualisation' or their goals and choices of life. This level would increase their passion and symphony, as illustrated in Figure (4).

Figure (4) Shows the Importance of Visualisation in discovering our intrinsic capacities.

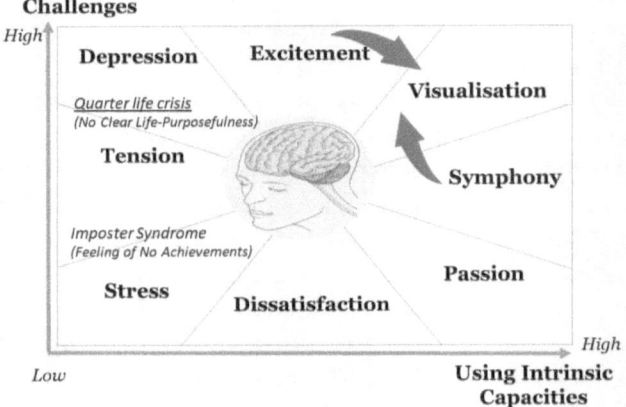

The framework encourages researchers and practitioners to use intrinsic capacities to pull the mindset of youth from negatively reacting to NEET situations to more consider them as sources of excitement of a dissatisfaction that raise the persistence and perseverance, the makes the youth passion and link it to their visualised life-purposefulness' goals, with a consistency called 'symphony'.

Conclusion

Setting transition and transformation focused research that enable NEET youth to increase their 'intrinsic capacity' is undoubtedly very essential for their quality of life and empowering them enough to be out of the poverty trap. Many youths want to come out of NEET or avoid, but the routes to such achievement are not always clear. Therefore, the key points of this research are to provide valuable insights on how to deal with NEET youth and eliminate their possibility in failing into a new type of poverty where their choices of life would be perceived to be limited. The paper suggests that if different practices set before-, during-, after-the 'zero status' or NEET as it called, then it would help to develop better life purposefulness practices that are driven by visualisation, choices of life, and focused decision-making.

Similarly, the proposed framework links practices that help to deal with the NEET youth dynamic situation towards using visualisation as a way to raise the intrinsic youth capacity. The implications of this research carry lots of ideas youth and NEET related mentors, managers and researchers.

As with any exploratory empirical study, the limitations of this research is that its data was extracted from one main project, the IIEP. Besides the framework proposed was built based on these data. Therefore, there should be more NEET youth poverty elimination projects in order for the results here could be generalised effectively. However, this research could open opportunities for more long-and short-term focused research efforts that could reduce the NEET impacts and highlights a new approach for reducing any possible future type of poverty.

References

Buheji, M (2019). Influence of visualised reflection on 'solving socio-economic problems' – a case from youth economy forums, Int. J. Innovation and Learning, 25 (1), pp. 1-16.

Buheji, M (2018a). Handbook of Youth Economy, AuthorHouse, UK.

Buheji, M. (2018b). Re-Inventing Our Lives, A Handbook for Socio-Economic "Problem-Solving", AuthorHouse, UK.

Buheji, M (2018c). Understanding the Power of Resilience Economy: An Inter-Disciplinary Perspective to Change the World Attitude to Socio-Economic Crisis, AuthorHouse, UK.

Brinton, M (2011). Lost in Transition: Youth, Work, and Instability in Post-industrial Japan. Cambridge, Cambridge University Press.

Carcillo, S., Fernández, R., Königs, S. and Minea, A. (2015). NEET Youth in the Aftermath of the Crisis, OECD Social, Employment and Migration Working Papers, no. 164.

Cox, S (2006). A NEET Solution, BBC News, Accessed 20 June 2019.

Elder, S (2015). What does NEETs mean and why is the concept so easily misinterpreted? Work 4Youth, Technical Brief No.1, Youth Employment Programme Employment Policy Department, International Labor Organisation (ILO), January. https://www.ilo.org/wcmsp5/groups/public/--dgreports/--dcomm/documents/publication/wcms_343153.pdf, Accessed on 20/6/2019.

Eurofound (2012). NEETs: Young people not in employment, education or training: Characteristics, costs and policy responses in Europe (Dublin). European Foundation for the Improvement of Living and Working Conditions.

Furlong, A. (2006). Not a very NEET solution: representing problematic labour market transitions among early school-leavers, in Work, Employment and Society, **20** (3): 553–569, September.

Hussmanns, R.; Mehran, F.; Verma, V. (1990). Surveys of economically active population, employment, unemployment and underemployment: An ILO manual on concepts and methods (Geneva, ILO).

ILO (2012). Global Employment Trends for Youth, International Labour Organization, Geneva.

Kraus, K (2008). Work, Education and Employability. Peter Lang.

Newton, B and Buzzeo, J (2015). Overcoming poverty and increasing youn people's participation. Crime and Justice Publications, UK. https://www.crimeandjustice.org.

The Intent

uk/publications/cjm/article/overcoming-poverty-and-increasing-young-people%E2%80%99s-participation, Accessed on 20/6/2019

- OECD (2016). Investing in Youth: Australia. Investing in Youth. Organisation for Economic Co-operation and Development. Prince Trust (2007). The Cost of Exclusion: Counting the cost of youth disadvantage in the UK. The Prince Trust. April. https://intouniversity.org/sites/all/files/userfiles/files/Prince's%20Trust%20Cost%20of%20youth%20exclusion.pdf, Accessed on 20/6/2019
- Robson, K (2010). The Afterlife of NEET. pp. 181–. In: Attewell, Paul; Newman, K. (eds) (2010). Growing Gaps: Educational Inequality Around the World. Oxford University Press.
- Shepherd, J (2011). Record Number of Young people not in education, work or training. The Gaurdian 24 February. Accessed 20 June 2019.
- Time (2016). Youth Unemployment an even bigger problem in US than Europe. Time.com, Accessed on 20/6/2019
- Yates, S; Payne, M (2006). Not to NEET? A Critique of the Use of NEET in setting targets for interventions with young people. Journal of Youth Studies, **9** (3): 329–344.

CHAPTER SEVEN

Reviewing Implications of "Poverty and Entrepreneurship" in Developed and Developing Economies[7]

Abstract

This paper reviews the work of Morris, M; Walter, J and Neumeyer, X (2018) published by Elgar and which blends two important issues poverty and the reality of entrepreneurship, which focus on the context of developed countries. The review first explores the book diagnosis of issue of poverty and its vicious cycles, through understanding the poor environment, status and conditions. The entrepreneurial approaches suggested in the book are evaluated whether they would find surely the best alternative solution for coming out of the different types of poverty.

The author accumulated experience of poverty labs carried out as part of the inspiration economy refine the review and see the entrepreneurship remarkable positive impact till the paper

---

[7] Buheji, M (2019) Reviewing Implications of "Poverty and Entrepreneurship" in Developed and Developing Economies, American Journal of Economics 2019, 9 (3).

reaches a conclusion with the proposed appropriate set-up for a future alternative framework for developing countries.

Keywords: Poverty, Entrepreneurship, Developed Economies, Developing Countries, Developing Countries.

Introduction

Emerging and developing economies are progressing day by day, despite many crises that are related to socio-economies and socio-political challenges. However, they are still late compared to the developed economies who have managed to bring in more effective entrepreneurship programs, Acs and Virgill (2010). All these economies besides developed countries are still suffering from different types of poverty and where the total percentages reach between 10 till 30% of the population or more. Morris et al. (2018), Powell (2008).

Poverty is not about lack of income or wealth; it is more about a complex multidimensional phenomenon — the complexity of poverty influenced by its current sizeable proportion. Relative poverty is even more complex. For example, in the USA, despite billions of dollars spent annually on poverty elimination, poverty communities are 14% larger than they were 50 years ago. Buheji (2019b), Buheji (2019d).

While some might argue there will always be poor people, their sheer numbers, and the corresponding cost both to those who must live in poverty condition in the larger society. In this paper, poverty is not just about lack of income or wealth, but in fact, it is seen as a complex and multi-dimensional phenomenon, Buheji (2019d). The paper goes beyond the issues of housing, education, health, transportation, family relationships, personal safety, job opportunities, career prospects and psychological and emotional well-being; instead, it focuses on integrating creative approaches that help the poor overcome their different circumstances. Banerjee and Duflo (2007).

In order to meet the requirements of reviewing 'poverty and entrepreneurship' in both developed and developing economies, we need to understand poverty and its relation to entrepreneurship. Then we review how entrepreneurship can be a solution to poverty elimination. Sachs (2005). Then we discuss the entrepreneurship clusters in poverty communities. Buheji(2019b), Morris et al. (2018), Acs and Virgill (2010).

Literature Review

Understanding Poverty

Poverty has always been related to GDP, overall wealth, standards of living and level of ownership. When considering what a poverty society is doing, we tend to think in terms of the median income rather than GDP.

US Census Bureau in (2015 and 2016) shows that the USA poverty is caused by the traditional setup of the minority of the wealthy people that are controlling 51.1% of income compared the other two classes: the middle and the moderately sized group at the bottom which accounts for 11.3% of the income only.

How Entrepreneurship can be a Solution to Poverty Elimination?

Entrepreneurship as a solution to poverty in developing countries. Alternatively, higher developed economics, where infrastructure exists, market opportunities can be significant. Entrepreneurship empowerment and transformation. It transforms market, industries, communities, families and individual entrepreneur.

The Intent

Involves a mind-set, a way of approaching life and the world. Pursue opportunities regardless of the few resources a poor person owns or control. Morris et al. (2018), Acs and Virgill (2010).

Entrepreneurship is a natural inclination of the poor. Poor themselves can create a poverty-free world, that we have put around them, these changes are powerful. Entrepreneurship is not something that is new among the poor. People who start ventures out of conditions of poverty. Many successful ventures have been created by the poor, given the complex burdens that come with poverty and inherent difficulties in starting a business. Banerjee and Duflo (2007).

Entrepreneurs pave the way to better high-potential activities that help to eliminate or eradicate or prevent poverty, Sachs (2005). If the poor starts to believe that they too can bring in innovation to the economy, notably the country economy would witness the great transformation and sustainable socio-economic development. Buheji (2019b), Buheji (2019e).

Role of Entrepreneurship in Poor Areas

The role of entrepreneurship is to excite the venture creation by the poor and reduce their greater gap struggle with those of higher income, or with a better education. Even entrepreneurship helps the poor to build more extensive networks, fewer health problems, safer surrounding and more exposure to entrepreneurial ventures. Buheji (2019a), Berner et al. (2012), Banerjee and Duflo (2007).

Moderate and extreme poverty remains a significant concern for many developing countries, Buheji (2019c). Therefore, entrepreneurship is counted on for achieving effective, sustainable poverty reduction, growth, and economic development programs. Reaching entrepreneurship by the poor depends on their level of accessibility for developing an active network, then they can and coop with the requirements. Berner et al. (2012), Acs and Virgill (2010).

In order to develop an entrepreneurship model that would fit the requirements for the low-income or poverty community, the critical role of opportunities recognition is examined, together with ways to expand the opportunities horizons of that poverty. Usually, such programs would be combined with literacy elimination, technology familiarity and community networking in order to build the necessary entrepreneurial ecosystem. As each relates to a person in poverty when trying to lunch a business. Buheji (2019a).

As the poor become entrepreneurs, they start to transform the economy and drive broader outcomes contributing to the global sustainable development agenda and SDG's Goal. These will result in the promotion of full and productive employment and suitable descent work for all.

Entrepreneurship Clusters in Poverty Community

Poverty community need particular entrepreneurship clusters that tackle poverty specific issues. Grameen Bank, managed to build a functional cluster around its concept of microfinancing for the poor. Grameen cluster goes on to diversify the type of credits for little income families and remove any collaterals that can be an obstacle towards their full entrepreneurship which may have no credit or low credit score. What Grameen bank does is that it helps the poor to obtain and access resources while also avoiding to fall into the "commodity trap". Banerjee and Duflo (2007).

Hence countries need self-empowerment holistic initiatives that focus on low-income entrepreneurs as they prepare for launch and grow successful ventures that entrepreneurship in its many forms offers promise to everyone in poverty. Cho et al. (2014).

The Intent

This means the real developed communities would be unique in supporting the poor to reach entrepreneurship potential without real barriers. Thus there is a need for a system that helps overcome the status quo solutions and make the poor create their own entrepreneurial pathways out of poverty. Morris et al. (2018).

Well-designed entrepreneurship programs improve earnings and livelihoods of the poor as it involves 'learning by doing' with efforts of 'income generation'. The poor are more fit for effective standalone programs more than any type of market activities. However, the poor needs business support programs that incorporate the most vulnerable and the self-employed and provide them classroom with technical assistance services tailored to their needs. Cho et al. (2014), Banerjee and Duflo (2007).

Entrepreneurship in Countries with High Poverty

Around half of those labelled in extreme poverty by 2020 will hail from hard-to-reach fragile and conflict-affected states, most of them in the Sub-Saharan African countries. In the meanwhile, Africa is witnessing a youth generation never experienced in recent history. Making the best advantage of youth in creating entrepreneurship would lead to proactive elimination of poverty. However, entrepreneurship in extremely poor countries, as in the Sub-Saharan which came out of colonization in the 1960s created a different model for their economic growth and development in relevance to absolute poverty reduction and employment creation. Buheji (2019a), Buheji (2019c), Berner et al. (2012), Powell (2008).

Africa has the fastest growing and most youthful population in the world hence the biggest workforce. Over 40 percent of this population is under the age of 15. Specifically, it is estimated that by 2050, the youth will constitute 18.6 percent of the population in Central Africa, 18.5 percent in Eastern Africa, 18.8 percent in

Western Africa, 15.6 percent in Southern Africa, and 13.9 percent in North Africa ILO.

Africa is also the largest continent with the highest number of people living in extreme poverty, which accounted for about 383 million people living with less than $1.90 per day, according to the World Bank. Generally, in examining poverty in sub-Africa, we consider of all sub-sharia African country. Buheji (2019c).

Across the planet, the number of people living in extreme poverty has dropped by more than half since 1990. The world managed to achieve a remarkable success stories in poverty reduction, Buheji (2019c). For example, China managed to reduce the poverty line to 15.9 percent from 84 percent (La, 2014), which led to sustainable economic prosperity development. However, almost all Sub-Saharan African countries failed to reduce their poverty below the $2 a day. Berner et al. (2012).

Once the poor in Africa become involve in the innovative entrepreneurship acts, they would upgrade their production capacity, and establish a high value performance that embraces continuous development and involvement of their communities.

Discussion and Concluding Remarks

The degree of poverty is related to the limited level of the capacity of the individual to create enough financial resources. If an individual cannot afford to pay for rent, or transportation, or health insurance, or to go to school, because they can't maintain self-sustenance or a minimum level of independence, then they would be considered weak.

Entrepreneurship brings in direct and indirect socio-economic interactions and addresses poverty, not as characteristic of a person, but rather a situation, Morris et al. (2018). Therefore, the entrepreneurship for those both absolute and relative types

The Intent

of poverty could also be different. When dealing with 'absolute poverty' where the poor do not have the necessary money to meet the basic needs of food and shelter we need to show them their capability to live the day with being semi-self-dependent. It is the necessary entrepreneurial skills and steps one in setting the mindset towards self-dignity. Here, the poor can see the opportunity for survival with more than the limited choices which they have been living on. Here even changing the geographic location, or the conditions around the poor, i.e. as treatment of illness or enhancing their functionality would make a difference. Buheji (2019e).

When we deal with 'relative poverty' we need to understand the situation of socio-economy and imaging the underprivileged cases within the society today and in the near future. For example, Buheji (2019 a, b) have mentioned about types of current and future poverty in the capital cities and amongst youth, due to the limitation of the 'quality of life' and the 'standards of living'. Therefore, the UK government defined that any household that does not earn 60% of the 'median middle class income' is considered to be in relative poverty. Once the poor starts to recognise the importance of their non-economic needs and wellbeing, they would use entrepreneurial skills to get out of his 'relative poverty'. Buheji (2019e).

Since income levels are highly related to relative poverty. Entrepreneurship programs that focus on the less fortunate should increase in a country where the income is high. This can be witnessed in the success of Grameen Bank in New York, for example, after its great success in Bangladesh mainly. Therefore, it is very important to address the individuals 'functional literacy' which prevent them from creating a complete deal. This functional literacy can be seen in generational poverty, where the individual experiences ongoing poverty for two generations or more.

In the same time, entrepreneurship can address situational poverty, i.e. when people go through circumstances such as forced migration, divorce, unemployment, or other source of life crisis, they would need an improvement for their life capacity and the way they would cover their life necessities.

References

Acs, Z and Virgill, N (2010) Entrepreneurship in Developing Countries Foundations and Trends in Entrepreneurship, Vol. 6, No. 1.

Banerjee, A. V. and Duflo, E. (2007) The Economic Lives of the Poor, Journal of Economic Perspectives, 21(1): 141–67.

Berner, E., Gomez, G. and Knorringa, P. (2012) Helping a Large Number of People Become a Little Less Poor: The Logic of Survival Entrepreneurs, The European Journal Development Research, 24: 3, pp pp 382–396.

Buheji, M (2019a) Eliminating Poverty Through Educational Approaches-The Indian Experience Review of European Studies; Vol. 11, No. 3; 32-44.

Buheji, M (2019b) Poverty Labs-From 'Alleviation' to 'Elimination and then Prevention', Journal of Social Science Studies, 2019, 6(2): 108-122.

Buheji, M (2019c) Re-defining Our Approaches to Extreme Poverty: An Attempt to Disrupting Contemporary Poverty Alleviation Approaches through Inspiration Economy Project-A Case Study, International Journal of Economics and Financial Issues, 9(4), 80-89.

Buheji, M (2019d) 'Re-designing the Economic Discovery of Wealth', a Framework for Dealing with the Issue of Poverty, International Journal of Economics, Commerce and Management United Kingdom 7(2): 387-398.

Buheji, M (2019e) Shaping Future Type of Poverty-The Foresight of Future Socio-economic Problems & Solutions-Taking Poverty as a Context-Beyond 2030, American Journal of Economics, 9(3): 106-117.

Cho, Y., D. Robalino, and S. Watson (2014) Supporting Self-Employment and Small-Scale Entrepreneurship. World Bank Policy 92629.

Morris, M; Walter, J and Neumeyer, X (2018) Poverty and Entrepreneurship in Developed Economies, E-Elgar.

Powell, B. (2008) Making Poor Nations Rich: Entrepreneurship and the Process of Economic Development, Stanford: Stanford University Press.

Sachs, J. (2005), The End of Poverty: Economic Possibilities for Our Time. New York: Penguin Press. xviii, 396.

PART THREE

FUTURE FORESIGHT OF POVERTY ECONOMY

CHAPTER EIGHT

Shaping Future Type of Poverty-The Foresight of Future Socio-economic Problems & Solutions-Taking Poverty as a Context-Beyond 2030[8]

Introduction

Introduction to Socio-Economic Problems Today

Today, the world is rapidly approaching seven billion people, while we are living and competing for more than ever in an interconnected global economy. However, this interconnected world still faces many kinds of complex issues relevant to safety, security and the challenge for sustainability which create pressure on the different socio-economic issues and specifically poverty. The issue of poverty is a serious problem to any country or

---

[8] Buheji, M (2019), Shaping Future Type of Poverty-The Foresight of Future Socio-economic Problems & Solutions-Taking Poverty as a Context-Beyond 2030, American Journal of Economics 2019, 9 (3), pp.107-117.

community and to the whole connected world, since the poor might negatively influence the economy, the healthcare, the energy, the environment and the education development (Buheji, 2018b; Ferrerira et al., 2017).

Despite the expectation of great decrease of extreme poverty by 2030, as the overall global welfare level is increasing; the deep gap between the richest 20% and the poorest 20% is expected to create other types of socio-economic problems. As the World Bank predicts that extreme poverty will disappear by 2030; one could observe a significant hesitation about what type of poverty would be really eliminated and what type of poverty would prevail and develop as a new organism (Wadhwa, 2018).

With the increase of income gap, where the capital economy would stay under the control of a narrow group, the poor community would stay deprived compared to the rapidly increasing welfare standards. This means that many individuals are expected to strive in the future in order to keep away from the poverty line (Buheji, 2019c).

In relevance to this understanding, the foresight of future poverty types requires that we study the history of poverty first, as shown in Figure (1). Then, we need to socio-economically understand and focus on current poverty problems projects, in order to visualise the future poverty problems and solutions.

Figure (1) Foresight for Future Poverty Problems Projects & Solutions

Study History of Poverty Problems & Solutions

Focus on Current Poverty Problems & Solutions

Future Foresight of Poverty Problems & Solutions

Current Poverty Elimination Success Stories

There are now many success stories that the world could show in relevant to poverty alleviation and elimination and specifically in the last two decades. However, there are lots of doubts about whether the same methodologies followed for such poverty elimination would be suitable for future types of poverty. For example, take the case of poverty elimination efforts done in China. The well-planned national policies led to the annual economic growth of 7-10%. The same was replicated to a certain extent with the many south Asian countries as India and Indonesia. The massive success of the South Koreans in eliminating their poverty came from their hard work and their fair distribution system. There are also countries who created success stories of poverty alleviation through the empowerment of small scale farmers as India, Latin America and Brazil. The other type of well-known success story comes from programs that address the poverty causes, as the Bangladesh program for reducing women inequality with the women-focused microcredit financing without collaterals.

These success stories were suitable for the eradicating extreme poverty of the past, where poverty community were always together and could be easily identified. However, the future type of poverty would be far away from such group absolute poverty; it would be somewhat more like individual relative poverty. If this proves to be accurate, this scenario is expected to push poverty from being a complex issue to being more of a complicated problem that needs to be codified, classified and then stratified with solutions for more specific cases and based on detailed demographic data or matrix.

Mohamed Buheji & Dunya Ahmed

How to Think of Future Poverty Solutions?

There are many reasons for poverty today that arise from the individuals and the communities' negligence, such as illiteracy, inexperience, and laziness. Moreover, there are many reasons for poverty beyond the individual and communities such as the management of the capital by a small group of people. If both types of problems would stay in the future, we should expect similar types of poverty solutions. However, we expect the future socio-economic problems would come from different practices. Buheji (2019c).

If we are to think of future poverty solutions, we have to go into the roots of such problem and think of pulling its causality in totally new ways. The concept of push and pull thinking in problem-solving is highly advised here. A push-thinking might be based on complexity theory, thus offering new tools for thinking about the future, while a pull-thinking might be practical efforts to solve the problems presented by changes in the condition of change, by inventing new approaches and frameworks. Any convenient socio-economic solution requires an explicit awareness of unique anticipatory systems associated with the logic of poverty (Buheji, 2019b; 2018a; 2018b).

Purpose of this Study

This study targets to investigate what type of future poverty-related practices and programs that need to be implemented or emphasised from today, as the world is transforming towards more relative poverty. The history of human poverty is studied, including poverty elimination solutions in religions, like Islam as an example. Then, the scale and impact of the future type of poverty would be studied based on the accuracy of the poverty data.

The study emphasises the importance of future foresight strategies to ensure that poverty would be staying at a minimal level and will not come in different type. Therefore, the author questions the feasibility of dollar metric as a suitable measure for future poverty and then question whether one could see that the world be poverty-free.

The literature review goes into the new universal philosophies that influence the possible types of poverty in the future. The social business concept of professor Muhammad Yunus is presented as an initiative of changing the causes of poverty under the current dominating capital-based economy. A visualisation of poverty future laboratories is reviewed along with the type of relative poverty anticipated in the future. The literature review closes with exploiting the expected deprivations that lead to future poverty types.

Literature Review

History of Human Poverty

Poverty was attached for much of human history and throughout all the world. The distant past had a standard of living that was very low in comparison to modern times, and this took 1000 years to change. Around 1500 AD, living standards started to improve in Renaissance Italy. Over the next couple of centuries, the centre of prosperity moved to the northwest of Europe. The Enlightenment led to industrialisation and incomes began to increase quickly.

Global GDP before 1800 was very low. However, by early 1900, prosperity had started to increase, and by the 1950's it starts in many places around the world. The world has changed dramatically since 1988 and is becoming more equal. For the last few decades, we have better data on global poverty (from the World Bank). Global extreme poverty declined from 44% to less than 10% falling faster than ever (Wadhwa, 2018; Ferrerira et al., 2017).

Besides the religions, the significant change in dealing with the poor started to be more precise with the Elizabethan Poor Law of 1601. The Elizabethan poor law of 1601 required each parish to select two overseers of the poor. It was the job of the overseer to set a poor tax for his or her parish based on need and collect money from landowners. The Elizabethan poor law, as codified in 1597–98, were administered through parish overseers, who provided relief for the aged, the sick, and the infant poor, as well as work for the non-disabled in workhouses.

Poverty Elimination Solutions in Religions-Islam as an Example

Islam has a shorter-term solution for poverty as part of the welfare share system. Islam emphasises transferring a small amount of the wealth of the 'high-income group' to the 'low-income group', through the obligation of the Zakat. The Zakat target to get rid of the poor people desperation and thus to reduce income inequality. Ahmad (2004).

In order to ensure equality in income distribution, Islam has set direct and indirect measures to overcome the huge gap in wealth. Ahmad (2004) mentioned how Quran praises those who can afford to give, only when they generously donate without hesitation. The promise of the reword of giving is ten times its value and flourishment of the livelihood. All Muslims who are not poor must share 2.5% of their wealth with poor people. This obligation should help to mitigate the harmful effects of income inequality. Kuzudisli (2017).

Zakat is not only an obligation from the rich to the poor, but also considered as an activity that enhances the legitimacy of

The Intent

wealth. Another type of obligation is the Waqef, where Muslims who can afford to grant some their amount of property or assets to the benefit of the poor or those in need for such asset. It is like sharing economy. These deeds should not be done as if it is a mercy to the poor, but is the right of poor people on rich people. Kuzudisli, (2017).

Scale and Impact of Future Type of Poverty

In order to create balance in protecting the poor from the social and economic instability and income differences, we need to prevent the opening of a gap in income inequality. Without this, poverty would always be a good source of criminal and terrorist activities. Therefore, Huff-Post (2019) mentions that the difference in income can be reduced by a certain amount of corrections in society's differences in economic income every year.

In order to understand the type of poverty in the future besides its scale and impact, we need to appreciate first the human wisdom and energy that each person carries within the self, regardless of his/her income, education and wellness.

Today, the world is doing fine in relevant to eliminating extreme poverty if we take from economic income, i.e. living above the US $1.5, per capita per day. The OECD and the World Bank reports confirm that now there are more than 64 countries who achieved above the first sustainable development goal SDG1 (no poverty) target, 12 countries have met the SDG1 target, seven countries are just below this target, and just more than 28 countries have gotten worse poverty than before the SDG1.

Despite this success, we still need to understand the future types of poverty and what are the structures and the practices that would ensure it will not come in more severe form. i.e. to move measurement of average income and go more specific about what is happening to specific people, regions and communities (Buheji, 2019a; OECD, 2013).

Therefore, codification and classification of poverty in the future should go into the details of demographics, i.e. one could expect poverty more in the ageing group those living above 70 years or more, where their constrained choices of life would enhance their feeling of living in poverty. Also, the poverty scale in the future could be related to the degree of freedom, rights, intellectual property and equality.

Future type of poverty would be expected to come from the rapid increase of urbanisation and globalisation. For example, Non-Communicable Diseases (NCDs), like obesity, diabetes, blood pressure, cancer and cardiovascular are rapidly increasing in many developed and emerging economy countries and are bringing in new causes and types of poverty in relevant to wellness and quality of life, besides low productivity (OECD, 2013). All these types of challenges are creating new risks for different types of future poverty that we need to mitigate.

Development of the Global Multidimensional Poverty Index

The Global Multidimensional Poverty Index (MPI) was developed in 2010 by the UNDP and in collaboration with Oxford University. MPI uses different factors to determine poverty beyond income-based lists, which is gradually replacing the previous known Human Poverty Index. MPI is an international measure of acute poverty covering over 100 developing countries and complements the income-based poverty measures by capturing the severe deprivations that each person faces. For example, the poverty deprivation might come from issues as lack or difficult to access at the same time concerning education, health and living standards.

The Intent

MPI assesses poverty with ten weighted indicators, which help to identify the poor and the extent of intensity in their poverty from ten factors in relevance to health, education and living standards. These ten indicators are child mortality, nutrition, years of schooling, school attendance, cooking fuel, sanitation, drinking water, electricity and housing. Even though these indicators considered to be an advancement in the measurement of poverty, not all of them might suite the future types of poverty. However, it is expected that some of these indicators would be used for the next 50 years to describe the characteristics of household and community.

Pro-Poor Growth Models

Pro-poor growth model (PPGM) emphasizes inequality reduction that occurs with poverty reduction during economic growth and takes into account both reduction in poverty as well as improvement in inequality. The implication is that while growth reduces poverty, it also improves relative inequality (Kakwani et al., 2004; Dollar and Kraay, 2000).

Kakwani et al (2004) seen that even though negative growth leads to increase of poverty, there may be situations where they lead to poverty reduction; if the effect of inequality reduction on poverty outweighs the adverse impact of negative growth on poverty. This negative growth scenario may be termed as 'strongly pro-poor'. This might an interesting concept that can be investigated in the future.

The monotonicity axiom is another pro-poor measure that the magnitude of poverty reduction should be in rhythm with the increasing function of the pro-poor growth rate (Kraay, 2003; Kakwani and Son, 2003).

Capitalising on the Accuracy of Poverty Big Data

One of the challenges of today and the future is the accuracy of relative poverty data. The OECD, World Bank and IMF have now big data for more than 134 countries. This data is claimed to be collected at least once every two years, but the focus was more on absolute poverty. The accuracy of these big data depends on the parameters it is defined to measure. However, the data is not enough to create clear visibility as the frequency is becoming slower than the frequency and depth of the effective decision making information needed.

The future poverty data accuracy is measured based on non-capital economy based measurements, i.e. shifting from a measurement of depending on US $ 1.5 / a day measurement to measurement of the ethnicity, the household composition and the specific region of the country where a type of poverty accumulates. This helps us to be more ready to understand future poverty in different ways. This makes us more realise what might be the different future sources that would trap people into deprivation.

Importance of Future Foresight Strategies

Unless we design and implement a realistic new strategy for disaster prevention, poverty problems might grow worse so rapidly and may reach a tipping point that would lead to an irreversible reduction in the quality of life of the majority of people in the world (Buheji, 2019b).

Hence, we need to anticipate and plan for the full spectrum of what type of poverty we would face in the future, so that we can build the capacity of the community for better monitoring and mitigation of poverty risks (Miller, 2018).

The World Bank, which was established in 1944 with a focused goal on how the whole world generates more income,

The Intent

without putting enough foresight strategies for the negative influence of this policy. Even though people living in extreme poverty reduced from 1.9 billion to 1.4 billion, this was based on the World Bank's definition, i.e. those living on less than a daily consumption of US$1.25. However, the roles of the poverty game are also changing, with more extremists, nationalists, coming up and more human-made and natural disasters are occurring with repeated trends.

Lately, the World Bank predicted that climate change would drag more than 100 million into extreme poverty by 2030. This means sudden environmental disasters, unbearable temperatures and rising water levels might drive millions of people of their homes. Hence, we might have another type of causes of poverty called 'climate refugees'. Other studies confirm that poverty would increase if the IMF and World Bank continue to emphasise their measure on GDP growth, regardless of the majority 'standards of living' (Kakwani and Son, 2003; Dollar and Kraay, 2000).

The Choudevsky work (2003) showed how the dollar metric is misleading. Displaced refugees, out of work youth, non-quality of life standards are all non-dollar metrics, yet they are highly influencing on future poverty. We need to visualise what structures of poverty we need to overcome in the future. This means we need to Imagine how poor people in the future, living in the compound of the less fortunate. Then we need to imagine what multi-deprivation they would need to overcome in order to meet the new life demands. This visualised future multi-deprivation need to be tackled from now as it is seen and observed from those who may come out of extreme poverty but still suffer from these deprivations.

Mohamed Buheji & Dunya Ahmed

Understanding Sources of Future Poverty

Poverty occurs when the world fails to address the needs of: people, community and environmental conditions. Poverty happens when we have instability in our set of habitats, livelihoods and social constructs or when experience unprepared recurring events as earthquakes or wars. Therefore, we expect future poverty to occur when we have an intersection between these three sources: people, community and the non-readiness of the recurring events.

Other sources of future poverty are linked to ignorance, apathy, disciplinary boundaries and unwise decisions. I.e. people would rarely see poverty due to chronic hunger and primary health care needs. We would see more of human poverty where the risk of migration is very high due to conflicts or terrorism. There might be an increase in morbidity and mortality, or homelessness due to economic losses from sudden and recurring hazards.

Due to the World Bank role in addressing the current sources of poverty, elimination of extreme poverty is possible more than ever and ensuring the welfare share by 2030 is more realistic. On the contrary, extreme poverty has decreased from 1.90 billion to 720 million. Despite these pleasing developments, the number of extremely poor people in the world is still high and concentrated in specific regions such as the south of the African continent and South Asia (Cruz, Foster, Quillin, & Schellekens, 2015).

The solution suggested for the elimination of extreme poverty ensures income per capita to increase a bit more. According to the assumption, poverty will decrease, as income per capita increases, and will eventually disappear.

If rich countries started to believe that getting people out of poverty, starting with their community, is not a moral agenda only, but rather an agenda that would ensure sustainable development for the concerned parties. This model can be seen clearly in countries where they wisely accepted refugees in the last years. Countries that as Germany and Turkey, accepted millions of refugees, yet their GDP has grown much more than in other previous years.

Poverty New Universal Philosophies

As GDP and income per capita increases, those with high-income levels get the most significant share from this development. Apparently, people whose daily income is not even a dollar have to wait for the further increase in incomes of those with high income to be able to keep alive. This brings in new philosophy about the possibilities of future poverty.

Equal distribution of income between households should be the main measure for non-poverty. As poverty becomes widespread, this creates a negative situation for all society. The status of the poorest 10% constitutes the portion of the poverty problem that should be resolved first and most quickly.

The future poverty is foresighted based on people will not be independent of the society they are living in. The society needs a series of corrections in favour of the future poor people, at specific intervals, if the free market economy is to stay. The fact that a poor person dies out of hunger would be in the future the responsibility of the globe, because future communities would be even closer, in communication at least, to each other (Buheji, 2019b).

Social Business & Changing the Game of Future Poverty

Professor Muhammad Yunus (2018) specified that old ways of addressing inequality through charitable efforts and government programs, cannot eradicate truly the poverty problem in the future. Yunus saw that we could solve future poverty only through actions that break away from traditional capitalist mindset.

The reflection of Yunus focused on how poverty as a socio-economic problem needs in the future to focus on eliminating the causes of poverty that start with greater wealth concentration in the hands of the few. The blame should go to something beyond interpreting human nature from an only capitalist economy perspective. Poverty solutions of the future, as per Yunus, should start by changing the assumptions of having them as labour working for others to have the poor as entrepreneurs, supporting each other. This shift on the thinking framework that Yunus (2018) proposed, build new economic thinking and help in addressing the poverty of the future (Buheji, 2019b; 2018a).

The adverse experiences that the world gone through hundreds of years should help us foresight the type of future poverty more clearly. Future poverty for most would not be created by the poor, but created by the systems, and hence it would be very logical to expect it to stay but with different shape and types (Buheji, 2019c).

Poverty Future Laboratories

The setup of the poverty labs is helping the world to know many things about poverty like what projects that need to be tackled, partnerships needed in the field before even suggesting generic policies that address the SDG1 main goal. However, all these labs do not address the future, it but instead focus on measuring ways to eradicate current types of poverty (Buheji, 2019a).

In order to build a road map for getting the future poor out of poverty, we need to assess their type of knowledge of what they know and what they need to know, besides their social condition. This requires action-learning research that brings in inter-disciplinary methodologies and solutions. Besides this, we

The Intent

need to understand how we 'use-the-future', in order to set up suitable Future Poverty labs (FPL), (Buheji, 2019a).

FPL targets to anticipate, discover and analyse the attributes of future poverty. FPL imagines and foresight the future poverty causes, practices and types and then start anticipatory activities that create basic models that make managing the future poverty more feasible and achievable. FPL, in short, tries to answer "what is the future, and how do we use it for the benefit of less poverty?" (Miller, 2018).

Narayan et al. (2000) and their team carried a type of FPL where they gathered views, experiences, and aspirations of more than 60,000 poor men and women from 60 countries. The work was undertaken for the World Development Report (2000-2001) on the theme of poverty and development. The work was titled 'Crying Out for Change' brings together the voices of over 20,000 poor from a survey conducted in 1999 in 23 countries. The other work, titled 'Can Anyone Hear Us?' also brings together with the voices of over 40,000 poor people from 50 countries from studies conducted in the 1990s (Narayan et al., 2000).

The Voices of the Poor project is different from all other large-scale poverty studies and helps to visualise what type of poverty, or poverty elimination related projects and practices we need to focus on. Using participatory and qualitative research methods, the study presents how do poor today and in the future view poverty and wellbeing? (Narayan et al., 2000).

Relative Poverty in the Future

In the past, there has been much debate on absolute and overall poverty, but now the focus is shifting to 'relative poverty', as poverty is highly influenced by the place and time we live in. Therefore, we need to foresight what is the relative poverty in 20 years from now, so that we visualise what we need to participate in the society in which we will live in the future. The foresight of relative poverty, help to set in mind the minimum standard of living to which everyone should be entitled to have to be above poverty in 30 years from now (Miller, 2018).

In order to visualise future possible relative poverty measures, we need to appreciate the other poverty measures used today. Besides, absolute and relative poverty, there are other techniques followed by different governments or international organisations to estimate poverty. For example, the UK government measure poverty line for those below 60% of median income. Another alternative approach to defining poverty is to look at the level of deprivation and what is the standards of living. Peter Townsend (1979), argues that deprivation should not be seen only in terms of material deprivation but also in the social exclusion from 'the ordinary patterns, customs and activities' of society. This applies of course to future deprivation too.

Part of relative poverty set by Townsend (1979) is the lack of resources that influence choices of lifestyle. Then we can reflect that future poverty threshold can be identified by the lack of necessities set by future standards and where the poor cannot afford it, i.e. not by choice. Therefore, one could expect that future poverty comes from multiple deprivations in relevance to future standards.

The 1983 Breadline Britain Survey and the 1999 Poverty and Social Exclusion (PSE) Survey developed the understanding of the influence of 'social exclusion on the poor'. The PSE covered the social relations, the labour market and service exclusion. The 'consensual' method, helped to develop the understanding of social exclusion and formed the basis of the current poverty and social exclusion research. The PSE approach could also be utilised for a more detailed understanding of the future levels of deprivation.

Meaning of Deprivation and Poverty in Future

Deprivation is defined as the lack of material benefits, considered to be necessities, in a society. Hence, deprivation is about living standards, which are a direct measure of poverty throughout history. Measures of deprivation are not the same as measures of income; they relate to how people live. Hence, one could say that 'future deprivation' could be defined as the consequences of lacking future income and other resources, which cumulatively can be seen as living in relative poverty.

Using Townsend (1979), relative deprivation approach, one could say that future poverty is about lack the resources to obtain the types of future diet and about the inability to participate in future activities. Townsend, developed sixty indicators of the population's 'style of living' could also be still suitable for future poverty. Even though his survey was carried in the UK in 1968/69, the indicators can still be used for future poverty: diet, clothing, fuel and light, home amenities, housing and housing facilities, the immediate environment of the home, the general conditions and security of work, family support, recreation, education, health and social relations.

Narayan et al. (1999) seen that changing poor people's lives for the better would continue to be inherently complex, because the lack of one thing never causes poverty. Poverty be it now or in the future would involve many interrelated elements, and the analysis reveals that without shifts in power relations, poor people cannot access or shape the resources aimed to assist them. Any poverty elimination strategy as per Narayan work needs consider four critical elements: (1) start with the poverty realities, (2) invest in the organisational capacity of the poor, (3) change social norms, and (4) support development entrepreneurs (Buheji, 2019c).

Such a study should help to explore the opportunities for enhancing the development strategies and ensure that it reaches the poor.

Methodology

Based on the literature review, a list of the current sources of poverty and future poverty-related problems published under the inspiration economy project were reviewed from Buheji (2018a) book on socio-economic problem-solving. Out of 51 poverty-focused projects, only 27 were identified to have the potential to stay as a source of future poverty, or symptom for poverty in the future. Each of the 26 types of projects has micro-projects that reflect the level of complexity (system based), or complication (individually based) approaches needed.

The 27 projects then plotted on a matrix to precisely specify the characteristic of each type of future poverty project, in relevance to the complexity vs the complication of the practices that lead problem solutions. The matrix shows that future poverty problem elimination projects tend to be complicated and less complex.

Case Study

Poverty Problems from Complexity to Complication

During the international inspiration economy project, poverty elimination related micro-projects were launched. Poverty in the future would shift from being a complex problem to be more of a 'complicated' problem. Complicated problems originate from causes that can be individually distinguished; can be addressed piece-by-piece; for each input to the system there is a proportionate

The Intent

output; the relevant systems can be controlled, and the problems they present admit permanent solutions. Hence, the complexity of poverty problem that results from the systems and networks of multiple interacting causes that cannot be individually distinguished due to the problem being with the entire system, is now going to be shifted to be more of complicated problems types (Meadows, 1999).

Thus, the future poverty solutions would be dependent on our capacity to work with closed systems, instead what used to be open systems. This means that the problems need to be addressed individually.

Distribution of Future Poverty Problems Projects

Based on the review of the list of future poverty problems solved as part of the inspiration economy project since 2015, the following table was set to represent both the type of projects which seen to be valid in the future and till 2030. The projects were carried out in the last four years carried out at different times and different countries like Bosnia, Slovenia, Bahrain, Morocco and Mauritania.

Only 27 types of poverty projects were identified in Table (1) and were plotted on a matrix, in Figure (1) based on the following criterion:

1. The project helps to transform poverty from being a complex problem to be more of a complicated problem that can be addressed solely, i.e. not dependent on system or other decision making circles or resources.
2. Each type of project has more than one micro-projects and practices that lead to poverty elimination in the short or long run.

3. Each project participants, directly or indirectly, in preventing poverty from occurring again.

Besides this three main criterion, it is worth to emphasise that not all of these projects have finished, or managed to bring precise successful results yet. However, these three criteria represent the methodology that integrates the poverty problem solutions projects with future foresight. This holistic approach claims to eradicate, or prevent all certain types of poverty, based on the changing lifestyle and latest world developments. Buheji (2018a).

Table (1) Summary of Poverty Elimination Projects that are expected to continue to tackle Future Poverty

Type of Project	Poverty Elimination Micro-Projects/Practices
1. Social Development	1-Inspiring the capacity of the productive family program to be more self-independent and attractive for more family members to join as full-time employees/owners. 2-Improving Quality of Life of Families in isolated communities and tribes (enhance the productivity factors for women and families working from home), with a target to reduce the impact of poverty through eco-tourism projects. 3-Building stronger family businesses that have higher Return on Capital Employed (ROCE). 4-Enhance the return from Elderly homecare production 5-Enhance the quality of life of the Disabled People and their Production 6-Easing the process of home care 7-Supporting 'Working from Home' Program 8-Revaluating the Capability of Social Allowance Value and Entitlement – in relevance to Quality of Life with priorities. 9-Enhancing the quality and competitiveness of the product of the Retired & the Disabled

The Intent

Type of Project	Poverty Elimination Micro-Projects/Practices
	10-Improving the Quality of Micro-Start Families with a focus on Women and People Vulnerability.
2. Psychiatric Services	1-Inspiration of capacity to manage the anxiety among the poor and avoid reaching the level of chronic anxiety 2-Reduce addiction and suicide ratio due to early treatment of main causalities among youth.
3. Labour Fund	Divert more mentorship on 'Necessity Entrepreneurship' and improve the solutions they bring to the community.
4. Woman Empowerment Programs	1-Closing the gap and accelerating the transformation towards 'Women Development' instead of 'Women Empowerment' especially among poverty and middle-class women. 2-Ensure knowledge sharing between Business Women, Women Entrepreneurs and Women of Productive Families Programs and especially those of the same or relevant business and link it to gamification rating. (i.e. Rating of Entrepreneurs who contribute and share knowledge)
5. Labour Market	1-Shifting Unemployment amongst low-income families through building models in specific industries and effective counselling 2-Raising opportunities for employment through sourcing type for job opportunities, especially in less demanding jobs
6. Social Insurance	Inspiring the social responsibility plans to ensure that particular type of lower pension jobs is more prepared for entrepreneurship after retirement.
7. Tender Board	Diverting more tenders to the benefit of local small SMEs and families' businesses
8. Housing Services	1-Reduce the gap between citizens' demands and their quality of life needs 2-Improving the choices and variety of options in non-villa packages (i.e. flats) 3-Reduce the contrary, social inequality and improve social coexistence through post-housing services
9. Police Services	1-Reduction of drugs trafficking through refinement and codification of smuggling through reclassification of information in poverty areas. 2-Enhance social harmony between neighbours for small issues among the poor neighbourhood

Type of Project	Poverty Elimination Micro-Projects/Practices
10. Woman Village NGO	1-Enhance the Return on Capital Employed for the villagers during the chain of making to delivery and distribution 2-Enhance young girls' involvement in Woman village activities to ensure the sustenance of knowledge transfer. 3-Enhancing the corps Return on Investment and profit margin. 4-Setting the type of transformation from distribution to start micro-packaging of high-end products. 5-Improving the quality of life of families in the Mountain Villages through eco-tourism and small family businesses that support such cluster 6-Build youth independence program that counters poverty through raising the capacity of the farmers for competitive packaging and distribution. 7-Build youth trust in the village system as a source of income
11. Migrants & Migration Risks Mitigations	1-Program for healing migrants' psychology and mental healthiness to create from them contributing citizens in the hosting country. 2-Help establishing special Entrepreneurship Companies (using collaborative & knowledge economy techniques) for Migrants youth that accelerate their preparedness for inclusion in the new labour market. 3-Create success stories of sharing economy based models of migrants who came back to re-settle and influence their socio-economy. 4-Enhance migrants' productive families' capability integration in the country of the host.
12. Women Entrepreneurship NGO	1-Analysing the impact of programs on 'woman development', not only 'women-empower', and the 'living standards' that comes with the 'Quality of Life' in the NGO area and scope of delivery. 2-Optimising the inter-disciplinary learning approach. 3-Enhancing the 'learning by doing' practices 4-Measure the differentiation of women on the economy.
13. Poverty Communities Transformation Program	1-Mitigation of Migration amongst Youth 2-Optimise the Youth Quality Life through Students Pull thinking targeted programs

The Intent

Type of Project	Poverty Elimination Micro-Projects/Practices
	3-Building a poverty blockage and prevention program 4-Addressing the Gambling (pitting) behaviour amongst youth and building prevention scheme through schools' model 5-Building Youth Entrepreneurship & Innovation programs 6-Enhancing Youth contribution in voluntary work. 7-Bridging the gap between academic Social Work and Social Studies Schools and the realised community problems. (Building Life Long Learning Programs that shape the Community) 8-Improving disserted women shelters returns. 9-Improving children without known parents' programs 10-Enhancing Red-Cross Programs Impact in the positive psychology of the community 11-Improving Pre-School influence programs on Children of Homeless and Beggars' families.
14. High Skills Craft Men & Women Working in Urban Factories	1-Transform the Factory-model from 'Production from the Factory' to 'Production to the Factory' by the productive families and women cells producing in their villages to maintain family unity. 2Re-Distribute the hand-craft Machines, hence the machines should be designed 'from being Factory-focused' to being 'Villages & Productive Families-focused'. 3-Re-establish Organic Handmade Carpet Marketing Program
15. Ministry of Labour	1Re-Engineering Counselling Services to start from High School and be Flexible towards Job Creators than just Job Seekers with particular focus on below middle-class families' students. 3-Help start-up companies that collect below middle-class graduate of unique, yet unemployed jobs, that as Nursing, Social Workers, Hospitality Services. 4-Nationalising Jobs that represent the country heritage and support tourism with below middle-class families related to these jobs. 5-Exploring the possibility of creating Human Capital Bank that would transform 30% of the Job Seeker towards job creation; over a planned career path.

Type of Project	Poverty Elimination Micro-Projects/Practices
	6-Closing the Gender Gap in Unemployment, by re-inventing new productivity jobs for below middle-class graduating women precisely.
16. Fisheries	1-Improve return on Investment (ROI) in fisheries and the resilience in the marines' food industry 2-Bring in the local market of traditional fishermen to sustain on the job with their families. 3-Establish National Fishermen Market. 4-Establish more by-products of fishing (i.e. shows, accessories, etc.).
17. Agriculture and Farming	1-Redesign Bahraini farmers' production by establishing what is called "National Farmers' Day". 2-Improve the distribution chain of local salad by attracting consumers to purchase local vegetables and fruits, and arranging deals between hospitality suppliers and local farmers. 3-Improve the level of Gardening Competitions
18. Improve the return of Endowments and trusts	5-Re-evaluating the current assets returns of Endowments and how they are professionally managed to support the people in poverty (directly or indirectly). 6-Establishing 'Sharing Economy' innovative practices and solutions to open more 'Returns on Capital Employed'. 7-Giving an innovative solution for solving problems on disputed family lands 8-Innovating on a type of endowments or trust funds to manage the technical and quality of life developments and diversify the resources in supporting the poverty community.
19. Bringing Low Privileged Community Children to Formal-Education by focusing on Sports	1-Integrating youth with both formal sport and traditional games 2-Evaluate possibility for the continuation of formal and informal education. 3-Use peer to peer education.
20. 'Education on Wheels' & 'Education at Door Steps' Projects	1-Target to deliver education to rural and isolated communities. 2-Formal and Informal Education for children in slums areas.
21. Improve the Quality of Life of	1-Improve Quality of Life of 'Waste Pickers' Families through differentiating their productivity from

The Intent

Type of Project	Poverty Elimination Micro-Projects/Practices
'Waste Pickers'	Municipalities coming to Waste Management 2-Segregating waste bins implantation in universities, schools & hotels, residential societies 3-Processing of the collected waste into high-end products (i.e. Metals, glass, papers, and organic wastes) processed to high-end products. 4-Improve the Nursery project and ensure the proper distribution channel of Nursery plants
22. Village Society – Productive Families & Eco-Tourism Program	1-Collection of small and large projects that target to create a comprehensive eco-tourism village. 2-All projects related to working from home and the provision of raw materials to making gift products, fashion design are inter-related, and this gives more importance to the project. 3-Target is to gradually make the village reach tourist spot with different hospitality activities especially during holidays and specific seasons
23. Green-house project in eco-tourism villages	1-The project involves many people from the village and youth to produce semi high-end products relevant to what the greenhouse produce. 2-Branding, Packaging, Labelling and Marketing of the semi high-end products of the eco-village. 3-Reduce Migration of Youth with more employment opportunities for the villagers' families.
24. Clean Water management project for villages	1-Addressing the influence of clean water on life development and as per the demographics of the village 2-Install long life water purifiers in the village and ask for labour work donation for maintaining the condition of the purifier.
25. Students Socio-psychology Awareness and counselling programs	1-Sponsoring project on counselling the students' social workers and councillors 2-Simplify tools for measuring poor students' safety or positive psychology, or stress release, or life challenges against continuity in education, even during child labour conditions 3-Awareness campaign for schools and universities, rights for the poor students and reduction school bullying, harassment of the poor. 4-Tackle issues of poor students' depression and see its influence on society.

Type of Project	Poverty Elimination Micro-Projects/Practices
26. Improve the return of University Courses to the Socio-Economy	1-Establish a model for Blanket as part of 'Fashion Design Course; in collaboration between the University and the underprivileged women
27. Anemia Prevention Program	1-Screening girls in villages for Anemia and link to socio-economic situation and productivity 2-Set preventive measures for future cases in the community with proper family planning. 3-Reduce the impact of individuals deficiency by addressing the proper diet plans, etc.

The type of projects listed in Table (1) was plotted in a matrix, in Figure (1). The figure relates complexity vs complication types of problem solution. The relevance to future poverty is visually represented in the 'top part of the matrix' where high complication tends to be the norm. The upper left side of the quadrant in the matrix represents the highly classified projects, out of the 27, that is focused on the future poverty taken the three criteria mentioned in this section.

Figure (1) Matrix of Complexity vs Complication of Poverty-related Projects

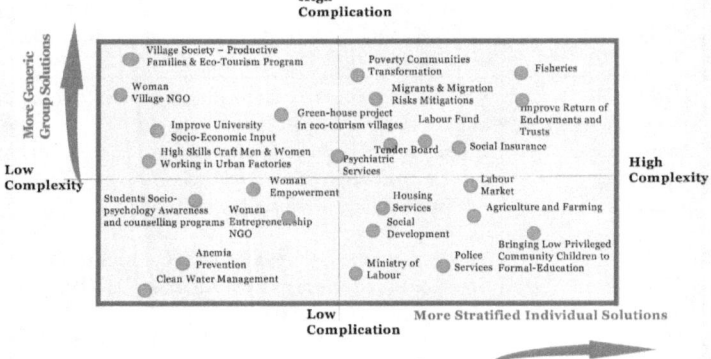

Discussion and Conclusion

Future Poverty starts with bringing those Behind

If you study the majority of those who are not catching with the SGD1 goal, you'll find them to described with one or more of the following: ethnic minority who have been marginalised by the ruling party, or tend to be more women, or most probably be living in rural areas, or living in the slums of the large cities. These codified groups need specifically targeted projects that are carried out efficiently with stratified microscale models (OECD, 2013)

Thus in order to bring those behind we need more today 'smart aid' than just 'good aid'. i.e. we need aid that helps to create stratified model solutions for the specific type of complicated future poverty than just an aid that targets to deal with complex poverty. This proposed framework of 'smart aid' not only it would address the chronic types of those still left behind in extreme poverty, but it would also be an excellent remedy for unpreventable wars or security crisis that occurs now and then in different places around the world (Buheji, 2019b).

'Smart aid' allows transformation change in a specific sector, or area, or a group that is lagging. Hence, based on the composition of the expected future poverty, we could design the type of intervention input. Hence, 'smart aid' would focus on 'bottom-up' empowerment approach rather than 'top-down' centralised approach. 'Smart aid' would deal with future poverty as an outcome, not as a status, i.e. a 'smart aid' would focus on eliminating women inequality that is leading to future poverty and future poverty-related issues as infants' mortality.

Mohamed Buheji & Dunya Ahmed

Changing the Future Poor Mindset

Poverty today is addressed from a particular mindset with particular social norms. The power of social norms mindset, like the way there are still what is called the untouchables in countries as India, need to be continually challenged and eliminated to avoid such poverty sources continue in the future in different means.

Another mindset that needs to be challenged and changed is the belief that certain people are lazy and need to be supervised and pampered. The assumption that poor people would stay not being capable of making wise spending decisions is another mindset that needs to change. Changing the mindset in relevance to the poor today and the future is not simple, but it can be done.

Future Poverty Action Research

Future poverty action research is about exploring the progressive problem of poverty and its possible solutions. This progressive exploration can follow either participatory or practical research styles.

With action research, we can improve the future poverty-related strategies, practices and the knowledge of the environments that lead to such poverty in the future. In this research environment, designers and stakeholders, along with researchers working with each other to propose a new course of action to help their community improve their work practices.

Future poverty drove action research could follow an interactive inquiry process that balances between poverty problem-solving actions implemented in a collaborative context with data-driven collaborative analysis to understand the underlying causes of poverty and enables future predictions, Buheji (2018a), Reason and Bradbury (2001).

The Intent

With action research balance between the researcher's agenda and the poor needs are addressed during the establishment and testing of the model solution. The research would be motivated by the goal attainment and the societal transformation that target to challenge the traditional social variables.

In future poverty action, research knowledge about the poor would continue to be collected through observations, as shown in Figure (2). These observations are then used to build the poverty elimination model. Then evidence on the proposed model solution would be collected and reflected on the next model. The research validity targeted would try to answer 'how to develop genuinely well-informed actions' that brings solutions to future poverty. We need thus to continue measuring 'relative poverty', which means not necessarily measure those living in low or middle-income countries, but also those living with the same proportion in the high-income countries.

Figure (2) Poverty Elimination Future Action Research

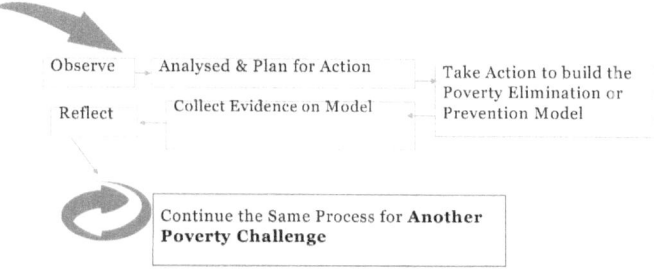

Changing the Poor Social Norms

When we view the world from the perspectives of the poor people, five findings stand out. First, poor people definitions of poverty include economic well-being, vulnerability, powerlessness, the shame of dependency and social isolation. Degree of dependency or autonomy emerges in many countries as a classification criterion of poverty. Poor people do not talk much about income but focus on the range of assets they use in coping and in overcoming shocks.

While poverty measures to today focus primarily on the consumption and the expenditures; education and healthcare would become the most important dimensions of poverty. Being poor would mean that there is still a concern about insecure livelihoods and vulnerability (Narayan et al., 1999).

Most of the poor who are not involved in agriculture find their livelihoods in the informal sector. Yet, most government and international attention are focused on formal employment opportunities. Poor people at the lower end of the informal sector lack any protection.

In order to come up with future poverty solutions, we need to understand what are the shared desirable behaviour of poor, i.e. the poor social norms. These norms can come from visualising the possible poor people interactions with landlords, traders, moneylenders and government officials. It might be understanding also specific norms as what women might encounter within the household.

Foresight of Future Poverty Problems

Sustainable development goals (SDGs) managed to bring to the world high interest in statistics and projects focused on dealing with extreme poverty as a socio-economic problem. Extreme poverty was collectively tackled from the stage when it was a problem in above 50% of the world population in the early 1980s and continued till today where it reached to having on below 15% in 2018 can be categorised to be in extreme poverty. The current trend of poverty elimination efforts shows that the world would continue to build equity in all sectors in the communities. This means that more international partnerships would be done to eliminate poverty through the integration of science and public policy.

Future foresight action plan and action research can take place from by specifying the types of future poverty projects, and based or the criterion that the project helps to transform poverty from being 'complex problem' to 'complicated problem'; where each micro-projects and its related practices would lead to poverty elimination or prevent its occurrence again.

In order to understand poverty in the future, we need to unders and what are the facts of poverty. Based on these facts, we need to study the possible positive or negative outcomes of poverty elimination and what window of opportunities need to be used. This means we need to find the right partners while gathering and analysing the facts, besides finding more selflessness driven problem solvers (Buheji, 2018a).

Fiel Miller (2018), see that people use the future to search for better ways to achieve sustainability, inclusiveness, prosperity, well-being and peace. This is exactly why we call for the foresight of future poverty. The way the future is understood and used is changing in almost all domains, from social science to daily life. The foresight of the type of future poverty can be visualised and anticipated today. The form the future takes in the present is anticipation.

In order to effectively foresight future poverty, we need to confront the concepts trapped in our mindset about today's type of poverty. This means we need to overturn the old frames and create new types of poverty frames. In such circumstances, we need to understand and overcome the poverty problems of today.

Although this research puts a new sport light on an area that is rarely studied, the only limitations for such research are it depends on the macro-projects of the poverty elimination efforts carried by the inspiration economy project teams. Further research in this line is highly recommended to address the future poverty in relevance to the micro-projects being carried out.

References

Ahmad, H. (2004) The Role of Zakah and Awqaf in Poverty Alleviation. Occasional Paper, 8. Jiddah, IRTT.

Buheji, M (2019a) Poverty Labs-From 'Alleviation' to 'Elimination and then Prevention', Journal of Social Science Studies, 2019, 6(2): 108-122.

Buheji, M (2019b) 'Re-designing the Economic Discovery of Wealth' a Framework for Dealing with the Issue of Poverty, International Journal of Economics, Commerce and Management United Kingdom Vol. VII, Issue 2, February.

Buheji, M (2019c) Shaping the Anatomy of Socio-Economic Community Problems towards Effective Solutions, Issues in Social Science, Vol. 7, No. 1, pp. 1-11.

Buheji, M. (2018a) Re-Inventing Our Lives, A Handbook for Socio-Economic "Problem-Solving", AuthorHouse, UK.

Buheji, M. (2018b) Recognising Lives around Socio-Economies? – Foreword, International Journal of Inspiration & Resilience Economy 2018, 2(2): 0-0

Choudevsky, M (2003) The Globalisation of Poverty and the New World Order.

Dollar, D and Kraay, A (2000) Growth is Good for the Poor, World Bank, Development Research Group.

Ferrerira, F; Christoph, L and Sanchez-Paramo, C (2017) The Global Poverty Update from the World Bank. https://blogs.worldbank.org/developmenttalk/2017-global-poverty-update-world-bank, Accessed: 1/4/2019.

Huff-Post (2019) How the world bank broke its promise to protect the poor? Worldbank-evicted-abandoned. http://

projects.huffingtonpost.com/worldbank-evicted-abandoned, Accessed: 1/4/2019.

Kakwani, N. and Son, H (2003) Poverty Equivalent Growth Rate, WIDER conference on 'Well-Being', WIDER, Helsinki.

Kakwani, N; Khandker, S and Hyun, H (2004) Pro-poor growth: concepts and Measurement with Country Case, Working Paper number 1, United Nations Development Programme International Poverty Centre. https://ipcig.org/pub/IPCWorkingPaper1.pdf, Accessed: 1/4/2019.

Kuzudisli, A (2017) Fight Against Poverty from the Islamic Point of View: The Wealth Distribution and Share, Economics World, Jan.-Feb. 2017, Vol. 5, No. 1, pp.9-15. https://www.davidpublisher.org/Public/uploads/Contribute/58171397c459a.pdf Accessed: 1/4/2019.

Kraay, A (2003) When is Growth Pro-poor? Cross-Country Evidence, World Bank Washington DC.

Lansley, S. and Mack, J. (2015) Breadline Britain-the rise of mass poverty, London, Oneworld.

Mack, J. and Lansley, S. (1985) Poor Britain, London, George Allen & Unwin.

Miller, R (2018) Transforming the Future, Anticipation of the 21st Century. UNESCO, Taylor & Francis.

Narayan, D; Chambers, R; Shah, M and Petesch, P (2000) Voices of the Poor, Crying out for Change. Published by Oxford University Press for the World Bank.

Narayan, D; Patel, R; Schafft, K; Rademacher, A and Koch-Schulte, S (1999) Voices of the Poor, Volume I, Can Anyone Hear Us? Poverty Group, PREM World Bank, December 1999

OECD (2013) Can We Really End Poverty? A Debate on the Future of Development. https://www.youtube.com/watch?v=VcQhRgho2ys

PSE (1983) Breadline Britain Survey – Poor Britain, ESRC research project, Poverty and Social Exclusion in the UK

(PSE: UK). http://www.poverty.ac.uk/pse-research/past-uk-research/breadline-britain-1983, Accessed: 1/4/2019.

PSE (1999) Poverty and Social Exclusion (PSE) survey, ESRC research project, Poverty and Social Exclusion in the UK (PSE: UK). http://www.poverty.ac.uk/pse-research/past-uk-research/pse-britain-1999,Accessed: 1/4/2019.

Townsend, P. (1979) Poverty in the United Kingdom, London, Allen Lane and Penguin Books.

Wadhwa, D (2018) The number of Extremely Poor People Continues to Rise in Sub-Saharan Africa. World Bank. https://blogs.worldbank.org/opendata/number-extremely-poor-people-continues-rise-sub-saharan-africa, Accessed: 1/4/2019.

Yunus, M (2018) Would Human Beings Survive Another Century? Dialogue Issue Newsletter (103), June, Grameen Trust, Bangladesh.

DISCUSSION AND CONCLUSION

Synthesis of the Literature: The Future Needed SDG1.

The world has been collecting its efforts to deal with SDG1 where currently all the known types of poverty are targeted to be eliminated or alleviated by collective efforts of all the United Nations-affiliated countries and non-profit organisations. However, the SDG1 is not concerned yet about the uprising and the future type of poverty, whereas many of the current poverty situations were not available 100 years ago, and many of the poverty situations would be different also in 20 or 30 years from now. With the speed of developments in technology, global economy, socio-politics and socio-economy, besides the increase of the frequencies of natural and man-made crisis; it is now highly foresighted due to such speed of the developments in digital advancements and artificial intelligence, we are going to move from witnessing absolute poverty to new and more complicated type of relative poverty. This is already clear in the developing countries.

Thus, the world would surely need a new SDG1 that set the framework for redefining the approaches on the way poverty is eliminated or alleviated. The future framework, Figure (0-1), suggested in the introduction is expected to help focus the field efforts in dealing with the poverty economy from assets and wealth perspectives. SDG1 would benefit from the collective efforts of projects that come from the different types of poverty labs and poverty elimination efforts on the ground.

Future Poverty Prevention Program

Education would continue to be one top projects that could be used in eliminating poverty, as mentioned in Chapter Four. The 'economies of neighbourhoods' and 'communities entrepreneurship' are excepted to shift the power of poverty prevention in the hand of civil society. Another example, on poverty prevention put forward in this book, is managing and eliminating the NEET youth, as failure to control those in poverty would create new complex poverty. The list of poverty prevention programs could extend to include sectors as healthcare, family productivity programs, improving the return of the capitals employed of those on the poverty-line, re-exploiting the wealth of the poor, social innovation and last but not least utilisation of behavioural economy in preventing any poverty-related diseases.

The last part of this book was dedicated to preventing future foresighted poverty problems that could increase due to the shift of the crisis of poverty from absolute to relevant one and in a rapid way. This part could be a subject of research for the thinking tanks, besides the practitioners who want to understand the underlying dynamics of the coming poverty. The world researchers are encouraged to work on shaping and determining the nature of future economic changes that would influence poverty instead of focusing on economic cycles only.

Future Poverty Economy a Multi-Disciplinary Problem

Poverty economy as a concept comes from multi-disciplinary backgrounds as economy, sociology, management, psychology, ecology, social psychology, socio-economy, economic geography, resilience economy, youth economy and inspiration economy. So does the future types of poverty economy.

The book shows the differentiation of poverty economy based on the future expected jobs and the capacity of the community to bounce back. Therefore, 'shaping the future of poverty economy' focuses on raising the capacity of the poor and their circumstances, in order to transform and proactively change all the welfare activities related to the poor and even the middle class, before embracing change. Therefore, this type of work focuses on helping communities to accommodate the new foresighted poverty.

The literature reviews show that future poverty economy could have techniques that are dependent on different monitoring systems that use field observations, called 'poverty labs'. The variety of the 'poverty labs' techniques presented in the book shows how governments, organisations and communities could deal or prepare for current or future challenges.

Future Poverty Economy might take many phases of transformation until it becomes relevant to the basis of social thinking. Today. The vulnerability of even the entrepreneurs and small business, is under challenge, unless the society embraces such proposed economy. As through future poverty economy, we can integrate human capital, with innovation and entrepreneurship to enhance the readiness of the relatively poor not only the absolute one.

Implications of the Book

This book is highly essential for re-evaluating the social development policies to make it fit the future coming types of poverty. The book takes more account for those that might be the most vulnerable after eliminating the extreme poverty and encourage more focused initiatives towards the relatively poor.

In order to sustain the effectiveness of the field efforts of 'poverty labs, ', we need more publications that help to share the success stories of the models achieved on the ground. This would provide more empirical evidence to remodel the current and future approaches towards being more adaptable to fostering more selective socio-economic solution to each type of foresighted poverty.

Final Words

The editors of this book have tried to follow a bottom-up approach, which means they covered the empirical studies of poverty problems and challenges from different backgrounds and different perspectives.

As a conclusion, one could confirm that there are ', no one size fits all' for the future types of poverty. Although a lot has been published about poverty, not enough has been covered about the role of Poverty Labs and how they could play a role in changing the formula, especially those coming as a result of the emerging work of behavioural economics and inspiration labs.

The recommendations are drawn based on the new different approaches shown to be of influence on the 'extreme poverty' policies and their ways of empowerment. The operational significance of the bookcases, in relevance to poverty alleviation and elimination, is that it follows the unstructured approach in dealing with the poverty of today and the foresighted cases of tomorrow.

BRIEF ABOUT EDITORS

Dr Mohamed Buheji is the founders of the International Institute of Inspirational Economy and *considered a leading expert in the areas of* **Excellence, Knowledge, Innovation, Inspiration, Change Management and enhancement of Competitiveness** *for over 25 years. He is a retired professor from the University of Bahrain. Besides being* **a Future Foresight Advocate. He** *is also the* **Founder of the International Journal of Inspiration & Resilience Economy and International Journal of Youth Economy.** *He has published since 2008 more than 70 peer-reviewed journal and conference papers and 17 books in the subject of the* **power of thinking, lifelong learning, quality of life, inspiration and competitiveness**. *Also, he has* **five books in English about Knowledge-Economy, Inspiration Economy, Inspiring Government and Inspiration Engineering, Resilience Economy and Youth Economy.** *He is passionate about transferring his + 500 consultancy projects experience for more than 300 organisations from all over the world, to both education and research. Also, he serves on the editorial board of 5 internationally peer-reviewed journals. He is a member of many scientific communities, journals, academic review boards. Lately, he is the winner of many awards including the latest* **CEEMAN best researcher award for 2017**, *besides being a* **Fellow of World Academy of Productivity Science.**

Address: International Institute of Inspirational Economy, [e-mail: buhejim@gmail.com, web site: www.buheji.com]

Dr Dunya Ahmed Abdulla Ahmed is an **assistant professor** and lecturer in the Department of Social Sciences at the University of Bahrain & **Strategic Planning & Development Adviser** in Supreme Council for Women. In addition, she is **Scientific Committee Chairperson in Institute of Inspiration Economy, EU & MENA.** She completed her PhD at the University of Warwick, to be the first and only person hold a PhD in social work in Bahrain, specialised and concentrates mainly on gender equity and the rights of people with disabilities. She is **the co-founder of Inspiration Economy concept, Journals, projects & institutions around the world.** She is also Editorial Board of several international scientific journals. Also, to being an active member of several NGOs & **president of Inspiration Economy Society** in Bahrain. She has also contributed to the preparation and implementation of several national strategies, and preparation and discussion of international reports.

Address: Department of Social Sciences, College of Art, University of Bahrain, P.O. Box 32038, Kingdom of Bahrain and Inspiration Economy Society, Kingdom of Bahrain. [e-mail: dr.dunya@hotmail.com]

www.ingramcontent.com/pod-product-compliance
Lightning Source LLC
Chambersburg PA
CBHW020645220526
45464CB00001B/294